Intended for Mature Audiences

Donna Thomas

W & B Publishers
USA

Intended for Mature Audiences © 2014.
All rights reserved by Donna Thomas.

No part of this book may be reproduced or transmitted in any form or by any means, graphic, electronic, or mechanical, including photocopying, recording, taping, or by any informational storage retrieval system without prior permission in writing from the publisher.

W & B Publishers
For information:

W & B Publishers
Post Office Box 193
Colfax, NC 27235
www.a-argusbooks.com

ISBN: 978-0-6922742-1-7
ISBN: 0-6922742-1-9

Book Cover designed by Dubya
Printed in the United States of America

Thank You

Love to Truman Thomas, Moo, Wendy Vance and Jacqueline, to my loyal and devoted friend, Tim Walkup, may you continue to recover and have peace! To the publisher, William Conner of W & B Publishers, all my gratitude for your patience with this project and your wisdom. To the editor, William Jackson, and a great cover by Dubya. Let's treat everyone a little kinder and better!

Intended for Mature Audiences/Donna Thomas

Introduction

On the thirteenth day of November, 2006, Timothy John Boham, formerly a well-known gay adult movie star, placed the barrel of his pistol against the head of John Paul Kelso, an equally well-known Denver Colorado businessman and pulled the trigger.

During the subsequent days and months, many rumors – some with a tinge of truth – and wild tales with absolutely no truth permeated the media that eagerly devoured the aura created by the cold-blooded murder. The details were juicy; a bright, handsome young star of gay pornography and a much older, gay, wealthy businessman. Lost in the fanatic frenzy that followed were the facts as to precisely what did occur, and why. What was to become known is that John Paul—J.P. to many associates—was found in his house, in his bathtub, dead and naked – and that Timothy John Boham was under arrest for murder in the first degree.

***

Who was Timothy John Boham? Was he just another gay performer, as many of his co-workers and legions of fans believed? Was he a devoted father who loved children and who doted on his daughter, as he had persuaded himself? Was he just a cold-blooded murderer, killing without mercy, as the Denver police and the district attorney tried to prove to the jury? Was he a delusional young man whose inability to cope with reality led him to acts of desperation and mayhem which he excused in the name of necessity? Or was he just a young boy who never grew up and was not able to take personal responsibility for his state and situation?

And who was John Paul Keslo? Was he a benevolent businessman, generous to a fault and open-handed to charity as many claim? Or was he a blackmailing homosexual preying on young good-looking men and insisting on sex in return for silence, as others said? Or was he a dominating dictator who drove his employees like slaves, as others—and the extremely high turnover ratio—are willing to testify?

Perhaps you, the reader, will reach your own conclusion and it may be that the truth lies somewhere in the middle.

Take a look at Timothy John Boham.

First seeing the light of day on May 27, 1981, Timothy John Boham grew up in Middle America; Stuart, Nebraska a town of 3000 people. Friends and family were quick to notice that

Tim was growing into a striking young man. Fascinated by the world of glamour and eager to make a lot of money, Boham, with the encouragement of others, sought to nurture his striking good looks into a career as a local male model. There was no magic rainbow; no pot of gold. Just a mere existence. Not satisfied with the mediocre success the local modeling jobs brought him, Boham looked for bigger and better opportunities, especially after he fathered a daughter whose mother died shortly after childbirth.

Now on his own as a very young single father, Tim headed out to California in a quest for the fame and fortune only Hollywood could bring him. What he found wasn't quite what he had expected. His ascent into a bigger playing field would lead Tim down a very dangerous path.

Author Donna Thomas, a seasoned true crime writer, introduces you into the life and troubles of a rising star in the adult film industry, with an interesting cast of characters that Boham encounters on his quest to rise above the corn fields of eastern Nebraska. Boham encounters the likes of the iconic pornographer Chi Chi LaRue, and big-time porn star Jenna Jamison. The twists and turns Boham has to navigate to mostly deal with his own deep-seated wrath leave him in less than stellar circumstances. He has a growing family to support, and must make the right decisions. Again no magic fairy. And – unfortunately – many wrong decisions.

Resolved to make a better life for himself and his young daughter, Boham abandons the good life in California for the more mundane life in Denver. While the money is not as good, Boham is certain that he will be able to make the switch. But events – including his own greed – prove that he cannot. Still, there is a possibility that he will be able to achieve his goals, but then he meets John Paul Kelso, who is not at all what he seems. And no one knows that better than an experienced crime writer who knows both parties. This is a story of small town values, evil verses good, relationship dynamics, the sometimes dark seedy underbelly of the adult film world.

Seasoned true crime writer Donna Thomas spent countless hours with the subject Timothy John Boham. Thomas had also worked for a period of time for the deceased John Paul Kelso. Ms. Thomas takes you on this sometimes very perilous journey of adult film star Timothy J. Boham AKA Marcus Allen as his thirst and hunger for fame and adulation explodes into chaos, love, loss and murder!

Intended for Mature Audiences/Donna Thomas

Chapter 1

Armed And Considered Dangerous!

Everyone, it seemed, was talking about the all-around great guy, John Paul Kelso. All the wonderful things he did for charity, his philanthropic pursuits, and a real generous gentleman.

He was the "life of the party," his long-time ex-personal assistant Seth Hill told 'The Denver Post'.

Seth Hill

Shock, disbelief, and a general sense of sadness **is** what many in Denver felt when they heard one of their own was met with an untimely and grisly passing. The news reports in print and on the television kept coming in. The short man, who had no known enemies – that anyone knew about anyway – was killed in the prime of his life. Shocking too was the way the man was found. He was found by his housekeeper, in his home. His car was outside in the driveway; as the housekeeper, Brent Cox, arrived for work.

Brent Cox

Cox had been Kelso's housekeep for the last ten years. At first it was twice a week. As the businessman became more pressed for time, the requirements increased the days from two to five. Cox was responsible for keeping the Congress Park mansion clean and tidy, as well as tending to the man's four beloved Shih Tzus while their owner was hard at work at his downtown Denver collection agency.

This was the home of John Paul Kelso, 'J.P'. to those that knew him. Kelso, was a 43-year-old white man, never married, living an openly gay lifestyle. He was a well-respected business owner. He opened Professional Recovery Systems, 'PRS' to those that worked for Kelso or did business with him – including his competition. He had opened the collection agency more than fifteen years earlier.

On this Monday morning, Kelso should have been at his downtown Denver collection agency, as he was every weekday morning. Instead, his car was outside in the driveway and his dogs seemed agitated and nervous as they paced around an outside patio area as Cox would recall a few years later while on the witness stand. However this Monday morning, Cox did not immediately become concerned at the sight of Kelso's car in the driveway, or even the nervous dogs. He entered the home through the unlocked front door. He did have shiny new keys to the home on his key ring. However, he tried the door first, and surprisingly it was unlocked. Cox was carrying his cleaning supplies he had brought with him. He started to call for Kelso to announce he was there.

As he called his employer's name and received no response, he started to do his cleaning. He noticed a few liquor bottles on the kitchen counter top, which he would testify was a normal sight for a Monday morning. Many times, Cox would see such a sight after a long weekend of house parties and overall revelry that Kelso was known to indulge in through the years. Even so. what was out of order – or seemingly strange to Cox – was that the house and kitchen were very clean, as if no one had been there. There were usually dirty dishes to clean and things to put away after a weekend. On this day, the house looked almost as Cox had left it early Friday evening, when he left his job for the weekend.

He stated that he sensed some feeling of alarm as Kelso's dogs continued to bark, yet he heard no sounds in the house. He went out the back door to have a look around the patio where the four dogs were. He immediately noticed the doggy door was shut, not allowing the dogs entry into the home as usual. He went up the stairs to the second floor which housed four bedrooms. Cox headed straight for Kelso's master bedroom. Seeing a lot of disarray in the room—all of the bedding was pulled off of the bed—he noticed dark stains all over the bedroom carpets. He recalled that he immediately recognized the stains as blood. He also saw what he believed was a bloody hand print on the white walls near the king-sized bed.

Cox felt dizzy and was having difficulty breathing. Instead of looking around any further, he dashed down the steps and out the front door.

He sat on the sidewalk and tried to gather his thoughts. He felt as if he knew what had happened, but felt that he needed to confirm his worst fears. He went back inside the house and up the stairs into Kelso's bedroom. He walked a few feet further into the master bathroom and saw Kelso naked in the bathtub with his face in a pillow. He later testified that he also saw blood all over the floor of the bathroom.

He ran down the steps and dashed through the front door of the house, onto the lawn. He took his cell phone from his pocket and dialed 911. Cox informed the operator that he was the housekeeper, he showed up to clean the house, as he had done for years, and found Kelso's body in his bathroom, naked and dead. The operator asked Cox if he was positive Kelso was dead. Cox responded in the affirmative.

Cox would testify that it was the fire department that arrived first, before the police. Then, shortly afterwards, an ambulance arrived. Cox directed all of the first responders upstairs to Kelso's bedroom. He was told to go wait outside, which he did, and was only outside for a few minutes when a marked police car from the Denver Police Department arrived.

The police took the now shaken Cox back inside the house to explain to them exactly what happened. He stated once again the same course of events as he had for the 911 operators. He was asked by the officers when was the last time he spoke to Kelso. Cox told the officers that he last spoke to the victim on Friday morning. He said there was nothing unusual about their discussion, just normal issues relating to Kelso's household, which Cox maintained for the wealthy businessman. Cox was in a state of shock, he recalled. Not known to him on that cold Monday morning in Denver was how exactly Kelso died.

Detective Nash Gurille from Denver robbery-homicide arrived to investigate the scene. Before anything could be examined very closely, Gurille had called a CSI team to photograph everything in the house, and especially Kelso's body in the exact state it was found.

After all of the preliminary evidence was gathered and documented, it was determined by a deputy coroner—who was now on the scene—that Kelso died of a single gunshot wound to the back of his head. It was surmised that Kelso had been moved to the bathtub after he was shot and killed. Kelso was 5'-6" and weighed over 300 pounds. It took six men to lift Kelso out of the bathtub. That gave the police on site cause for concern; they wondered how many people were behind Kelso's murder. They believed at first it was far more than one assailant, as the possibility of only one person putting him in the bathtub was almost impossible.

A full-fledged investigation was in motion to find a suspect in Kelso's murder. On the news, it was being reported that Kelso was more than likely a victim of a home robbery. There was no mention of the manner in which Kelso was found—or by what means he was murdered—just that he was murdered. People were being asked via the media to contact Crime Stoppers with any information about Kelso's murder.

For whatever reasons, I had not heard anything in the media regarding Kelso's death. I am certain that I didn't because it was a mutual friend of ours who informed me that Kelso – a man for whom I once did legal work – was dead. The friend that informed me of Kelso's death was Tim Walkup, who also owned a collection agency in Denver. He did business with Kelso on a regular basis. He knew him; he didn't consider him a friend but a business associate that he felt he knew well. He called me on the Saturday before the police state the body was found.

Tim called me on a Saturday evening late. I remember it was after midnight. He said "Guess who died?"

I said, "Who?"

He said, " J.P. Kelso."

I didn't believe him at first. I think most people are taken aback when notified someone that they know is gone, and the person was not elderly or ill. However, even though I was verbally saying I wasn't sure I believed Kelso was dead, I think mentally and emotionally I knew very well that Kelso was indeed dead.

***

On the other side of town from where Kelso's body was found lived a woman named Susan Strong.

She was a wife, mother, sister, daughter; she had two children at the time of Kelso's death; a son the family called John, age 25, and his older sister Kathrynne, age 27. Her son John was a model and father of a five year old daughter Jasmine Boham.

Susan Strong

Susan Strong was originally from the small town of Stuart, Nebraska. Susan's late husband—the father of her two children—died in truck driving accident when John was 13.

Susan went on a business trip to Denver, met a man named Walter Strong, the two hit it off immediately. A very short time later they would marry. The family relocated to Denver about 10 years before November of 2006.

**

After reviewing several pieces of evidence, such as Kelso's phone and computer records, the police had a suspect. They were now looking for a 25-year-old man; they believed he was the last person to see Kelso alive. They also said that the suspect was a former gay porn actor. They didn't say too much more than that. They did say they believed the suspect should be considered armed and dangerous. They went on to say their standard admonishments that no one should approach the suspect if they see him, but rather call the police.

The Denver Police Department was working tirelessly to bring the suspect in, and provide some level of peace to the victim's family. They weren't sitting on their laurels, just waiting for the suspect to jump in their laps. They went over to Susan Strong's home, hoping against hope her son John would be there. They came armed with tools to help identify Strong's son John. Two undercover Denver police detectives appeared on the doorstep of Susan and Walter Strong's Denver home some ten days after Kelso's naked body was discovered in the bathtub of his home.

Susan Strong answered the door. Mrs. Strong believed at that moment her son John was in

Los Angeles working on a modeling shoot. The men standing in front of her identified themselves by showing her their police badges. They asked if her son, 'Marcus Allen' was there. She responded to the strange question by saying, "I don't have a son named that, his name is John". They asked if she knew a Marcus Allen, she responded that she did not.

She allowed the men inside of her home and naturally became extremely nervous. She may have had some idea that her son was in a bit of trouble, as he appeared at the same home only a week or so before this night. She wasn't letting on that she had a vague idea as to why the detectives were now in her living room. If she had a germ of an idea as to the police visit, it was only about what had transpired in Denver a week or so before. That was her only knowledge on this night. She was in for the shock of her life.

The police asked Susan Strong what her son's full legal name was. She responded with "Timothy John Boham." They asked her where did she believe he was at that moment. She said that he was in Los Angeles on a modeling shoot. They asked Mrs. Strong, what company her son was modeling for. She couldn't not answer them with specifics; she indicated she thought it was a jean company.

They asked Susan Strong, if she had a VCR or a CD player in her home. She responded that she did, and pointed to the front of the room where a small entertainment center stood. One of the detectives stood up and said "May I?". She nodded in the affirmative, the man took out a CD from a plastic evidence bag and put it in the CD player. As the credits started rolling, Susan Strong was now joined by her husband, Walter Strong, John's stepfather. The film, *'Road To Temptation',* started to play in the living room of this extremely religious Christian family. A family that rarely missed a Sunday service was now sitting with two detectives from the Denver Police Department, horrified as they began to watch a hardcore gay porn film. The detective started to fast-forward the film, stopped it, and instructed Susan Strong to look closely at the man in the frame. He asked her if that was her son, John.

She said, "It looks like him, but it just can't be him."

He said, "Ok we will resume playing it, because he has a few lines here. Listen to his voice, please. The film started to play again, and Timothy John Boham, appearing as 'Marcus Allen', was on film. Mrs. Strong started to weep uncontrollably as she sat horrified, listening to the voice of her beloved son, John, as he was called by his family.

She shouted to the officers to stop the tape. "Stop the tape, stop the tape, I've seen enough, please stop it!"

The detective knelt down in front of Susan Strong. He proceeded to ask her if that was her son on the tape. He said, "Is that your son, Ma'am?"

Timothy John Bohan

She shook her head from side to side, and was crying so loudly, that she was not audible. Her husband Walter told the police that, "Yes, that is my stepson, John Boham."

He asked the officers what they could do right now to help the police. One detective sat back down on a couch directly across from Susan

Strong, and said, "Ma'am, your son was involved in the porn industry. He made several films, and we're trying to determine if that has anything to do with a crime we are investigating. Right at this moment we have to find him. We have a warrant for his arrest for the first degree murder of John Paul Kelso."

The police asked her when was the last time she had talked to her son. She said, "About 5 days ago." She, along with her husband, said they wanted to talk to her brother before they said anything more. Susan Strong's brother was a retired Colorado police officer. The detectives handed Susan their business card and asked her to call immediately with anything regarding his whereabouts, and urge her son to turn himself in, "So that he doesn't get killed out there."

She looked at the police officers in a very confused way.

One of them responded to her, "Well, he is considered armed and dangerous. Unless he is in police custody anything is possible. Tell him to turn himself in; he's making everything worse for himself." The officers got up, headed to the front door and left the house.

Mrs. Susan Strong collapsed on the carpeted floor, praying that what they had just told her about her son John was not true.

***

Oh, but it was true, every word of it! The next few years would bring about more and more information about her son, his life and his demons. She would have to deal with a lot more than most people would be able to cope with. She believed that her son was straight, a hardworking model.

He was a father to a five-year-old girl—her beautiful and only grandchild—and he also currently had a beautiful, pregnant girlfriend.

However the police had just told her that her son was wanted for the capital offense of first degree murder. She also learned that her son had been doing gay porno films; not only was she told, but shown that fact in living color on the family television set in the living room. The same set that broadcasts religious lectures and specials with predictable regularity.

***

It would be a very long arduous road for the family of Timothy John Boham. It would leave not only Bonham's family irrevocably changed, but a community of like-minded business professionals, family, and friends of the victim shaking their heads in disbelief. An interesting cast of characters would start to emerge as the circumstances of the murder of John Paul Kelso, known by friend and foe as' J.P', would start to unravel.

****

It starts in Stuart, Nebraska, a town today that only has some three thousand residents; everyone knows everything about everyone else. The story would make a detour in the mile-high city, Denver. It would make several stops, twists and turns in Southern California, home to the majority of adult film productions. The story will take tragic turns and end so horrifically in Denver, and come to its final resting place in Canon City, Colorado. It's a cautionary tale, but is it really?

Chapter 2

Humble beginnings in Stuart, Nebraska!

The zodiac sign of the Gemini, is reserved for all the people born between the dates of May 21 to June 21. There are some very impressive people born under the sign of Gemini. Included among this illustrious group are the great builder Cornelius Vanderbilt; former Secretary of State during the Nixon administration, Henry Kissinger; Wild Bill Hickok, a very well respected lawman and army scout of the American Great West—who had quite the reputation during the 1800's until his death in 1837.

Lisa "Left Eye" Lopes of the highly successful 90's girl band, 'TLC' was born under the Gemini sign. As was the late actor Vincent Price, most noted for his propensity of playing ghouls and ghosts.

Academy Award winning actor Louis Gossett, Jr. and Todd Bridges also are under the sign of Gemini.

These people are not only Gemini's, but they all share another little factoid, they have the same birthday, May 27th. Another man joins this group that have the birth date of May 27th.

Timothy John Boham was born on May 27th, 1981, in Omaha, Nebraska. His natural parents were Susan and Tim Boham. Tim Junior—or 'John' as he has been called by his family—joined his two-year-old sister, Katheryn Boham, and that completed the All-American mid-western family.

However looks can sometimes be very deceiving.

TIMOTHY BOHAM

Tim's parents, Susan and Tim, were frequently engaged in huge arguments and things were really less then picture perfect. The senior Tim Boham liked to use different members of his family as the proverbial punching bag. They were each the object of his disdain at any given moment.

Susan Boham was a woman deeply devoted to her Christian faith. She was a regular churchgoer, and more times than not she brought young John and Katheryn with her to be involved in all the services and activities of the church. She had resettled in the mid-west, after spending her youth in Philadelphia. She was married to a very volatile man, this Tim Boham. He and Susan would continuously have long battles, late into the night and into the morning. Not the most stable of environments to raise two small children. He would grow angry with his wife and two young children. His answer was a belt, a chair, the back of his hand; everything and anything he could grab, hold or pull is what he used on his family.

He also had a chronic and severe drinking problem, complete with black-outs. Tim Senior was a long-distance truck driver for a major trucking firm. That type of career choice left Susan and her children alone in Nebraska for weeks at a time. However, the long absences from the family gave some sort of reprieve from the constant battling and rages that were common place in the Boham household. Susan,

Timothy Junior and Katheryn all claim years of endless abuse, both physical and verbal, by Tim Senior. They say he was quite relentless in his tirades against them. Susan, Timothy's mother, would recall that her husband could be provoked at the drop of a hat. She said there was no rhyme or reason to his attacks, however, it was an established fact that he was prone to fits of rage that could last hours or days, as Susan recalled what life was like in Stuart, Nebraska, in the mid 1980's. The Boham's certainly didn't have an easy time in the middle of the farm belt. Money was always in short supply to add even more pressure to their volatile situation in the home front.

In addition to the senior Boham's temper, he had a severe drinking problem. What little extra money there was never lasted very long, and usually was spent on bottles to further fuel the senior Tim's raging temper. Many in the inner circles have said that when the senior Tim was on the road he had various women in different cities that he was spending money on. That even created further conflicts at home when he would return. When he did arrive at home he could be extremely moody and sullen and very agitated. It was an extremely tumultuous environment for the children to grow up in.

There were always rather caustic eruptions in the Boham household at the drop of a hat. For a young child such as little Timothy John Boham, the memories of his cantankerous father would create indelible impressions with repercussions that are open to interpretations.

Susan, young Tim's mother, was a deeply religious woman. She may have used religion as a crutch, as some have suggested. Perhaps a vehicle of escape from her less the ideal circumstances. She had the church, a place that in the past had always offered her a great form of solace and hope. When things were toxic in her home, the church literally functioned as a place for refuge, for herself and her two young children, young Tim and Katheryn.

Tim Boham recalled being brought to church on a regular basis, "Like it or not, that's what you did. You went to church." He disliked it a lot more then he liked it. However, even for young Tim, it could offer him a safe place. A place where he couldn't be screamed at, or needlessly hit and tormented by someone he loved and trusted.

Although young Tim loved and trusted his very authoritative father, he recalled that he feared him more than anything else. He said of those days, "You just never knew what would set him off. The worst part," Tim would go on to say, "The worst part of all is that it wasn't any one thing that you could pin-point that would be a trigger to my father's outbursts."

In order to make ends meet in the Boham household, Susan would try to pick up odd jobs, like sewing, and cooking for friends and neighbors. However, worries over money were constant issues that always had everyone in the house on edge, including the young Boham children. Tim said of those days, "Kids shouldn't have to know about the money troubles of their parents, but I always knew." A tell-tale sign of things to come in Tim Boham's future???

***

Young Tim was a very small boy—always the smallest in his classes—throughout the majority of his years in the public school system. He was the object of a lot of harassment, and says that he felt tormented by just about everyone else. He recalled, "It was always the same kids, that did the teasing. The same ones that laid into me in first grade continued all the way to high school. I hated everything about school."

Young Tim would move through his elementary school grades with relative ease. Being smaller than most didn't stop the rather rambunctious Tim Boham from making friends and being very delightful, according to many of the teachers. He would be diagnosed with hyperactivity when he was eight and in the third grade. Susan and her husband Tim Senior decided that little John, as he was called by the family, would not seek out medication. The family was hoping that the disorder would wane as Tim grew older.

Tim's father was involved in a very bad accident in his big rig. It happened in 1994, when Tim was 13 and in junior high. The accident occurred only 20 miles away from the Boham home and after Tim Boham had been gone for over two weeks. The roads in Nebraska at that time were very icy, and Tim's father's vehicle skidded and jumped the medium, and plowed into oncoming traffic. He would die a short time later in the hospital.

Life for the Boham's was now about Susan and her two young children. It was about providing them with the skills and financial resources to help pave the way for their own successful relations with others. Life was never easy in this eastern part of Nebraska for Susan, but with the elder Tim Boham gone, all of them agreed that their lives were—to a certain point—much more peaceful. Gone was the maniacal, merciless Tim Boham Senior. The two Boham siblings were starting to realize that anything is possible, and to dream big. After the death of Tim's father, life would never again be the same for those he left behind, but they felt they were left with nothing, sadly, even though their mother was encouraging to her young children.

Tim's dreams of an acting career, or being a model were starting to flourish during the time of his father's passing. He got hit hard with the 'acting bug'. He—along with his peers—knew that in order to really get anywhere in life, one needed to expand their horizons. In this case, the town of Stuart was about 165 miles from nowhere. So, in order to have any chance and exceed in life, everyone knew that the chances were you weren't going to be staying around Stuart and became a raging success. All Tim John Boham knew was that he didn't want to live the way his family did, always scrambling around for a few extra dollars, or even never being able to make ends meet. He wanted success, and knew it.

Timothy John Bohan

Chapter 3

Branching Out

Tim, along with the rest of the Bohams, was coping with death of the senior Tim Boham. Life was different after his father's death. Susan would recall, "But different is sometimes very healthy."

Tim had discovered acting around this same time period. He started to audition for a few school plays at Stuart High School, and actually was cast in a few parts. At about this time, Tim also discovered girls and they discovered him. This same Tim Boham, who was regularly tortured by the older and bigger boys at school, was now becoming known as 'quite the ladies' man'. He was now very admired by the entire student body for his ability to get the most attention. He would grow into his looks at over 6 feet tall, with All-American boy-next-door good looks. People, both males and females, were very much starting to notice young Timothy John Boham.

Timothy John Boham

***

Intended for Mature Audiences/Donna Thomas

One day, a new girl arrived at Stuart High School and her name was Monica. She was a very striking, ebony-skinned girl of 5'-5." Monica, along with her two younger siblings and mother, had moved to the tiny rural town from Lincoln, Nebraska. Her mother was going through a difficult divorce from Monica's stepfather, her second husband. Her daughter's world was being shaken up and down and sideways.

Monica had a hard time fitting in at Stuart High School, which only had just a few students of color. Someone like Monica stood out like a sore thumb in the predominately white school. At first it was very hard for Monica to feel as if she fitted in, or even feel a part of the community there. Tim Boham met Monica on her very first day at her new high school. She was lost and asked Tim for directions to her science class and Tim gave them to her, but not before he asked her name!

He let Monica know that there were good people at Stuart High, and if she ever needed a friend, he would be there for her. A little much for just having met someone? According to Tim, "She was so different from the average ho-hum Stuart, Nebraska. I was really starting to rebel against everything that reminded me of me, if that makes sense, and she certainly was very far from what I was, and because of that, she was the most exciting thing that ever happened to me. I was just determined to get to know her!"

Get to know her he did. and the two very quickly became inseparable. They were together all the time, and started to date exclusively, and call each other 'boyfriend' and 'girlfriend'.

Tim would reminisce about his early days with Monica, and how he thought the relationship had developed into something quite deep very quickly. He said he felt he had a lot in common with her; him dealing with the loss of his abusive father, she the absence of her abusive stepfather. They both felt they had a lot in common and could relate to each other. Tim has told me he felt with Monica he could let his guard down, and really strive for great—not mediocre—but great. At this juncture Tim asserts he was just an occasional pot smoker. He and Monica smoked pot regularly, and sometimes would skip school and just hang out all day at one of their homes, and watch TV and eat and get high. He said they were pretty innocent times, and he didn't realize at the time how he would miss it when it was gone.

He also remembered that pot was all he ever knew Monica did. He would later learn that this wonderful girl that he was falling in love with was also into much harder drugs, like coke and prescription pills she stole from her mother. Once he learned the truth about his now girlfriend, it really shocked and disappointed him at the same time. He would try to get her to quit her various addictions, but to no avail.

Drugs aside, both Tim and Monica had goals, and they both dreamed big. They really believed they could both be rich and famous. Lofty goals perhaps, but the two of them were certain that the golden ring was within their reach. He wanted to be a famous actor, and Monica had long ago caught the fashion bug, and wanted to design the latest and fashions that only the most beautiful people in the world would wear.

One thing that the two lovebirds felt they needed to do was convince those around them that they were meant to be together. Constant backlash from their respective families caused the two constant anguish and stress, even at their very young ages. Tim was quite certain his family, namely his mother Susan, just didn't approve of Monica because she was black. Monica's mother just didn't want her daughter to become pregnant. She wasn't concerned about anyone's color. Monica's mother became a mother as a teenager and she desperately was trying to stop that cycle with her own daughters.

Several years later, Susan recalled that Monica's color was of no concern to her. What concerned her was Monica's rampant drug use. Tim did confide in his mother when it came to things that were troubling to him about his relationship with Monica. His girlfriend, he would learn, inherited her penchant for all things drugs from her biological father, who was also a tireless drug addict. He would do anything he could to get his hands on, and never seemed to be able to quit.

Tim would repeat that he was never into anything harder than pot, back then or ever. He truly never realized that Monica was into anything harder then pot until he was madly in love with her. She kept her addictions a hidden secret from her boyfriend. Breaking up with Monica over her addictions was not something Tim was ready to consider.

Heading into their senior year of high school, Susan Boham met a man from Colorado, Walter. They would eventually marry and move to Denver, Colorado. Tim and Kate Boham, were now 17 and 19 respectively. The two teenagers decided it was in both of their best interests to move with their mom to Colorado. Tim at this point only had a few more months of high school to go. He decided to leave school in lieu of the upcoming move, and he did eventually take a GED exam and pass it. He was sad to leave his girlfriend Monica in Stuart, but though it was ending, it was enabling him in securing both their futures in a bigger place that offered opportunities that were just not attainable in a town of three thousand people.

***

The Boham children were now residing with Susan and Walter Strong in Aurora, CO, which is a suburb of Denver. Almost immediately young Tim became aware of the opportunities that this mile-high metropolis offered him. He quickly became inebriated with the mere thought of everything that was now available to him; things that he had no clue about while living in a town of a couple thousand people. To this now young man of 18, the thought of what could be was quite intoxicating to him. He also felt that any dreams of becoming known and successful was much more attainable now.

Monica was still in Stuart, Nebraska, finishing up her senior year of high school. The two high school sweethearts still saw each other. However they were now 460 miles away from each other. Occasionally Tim, would make the seven-hour drive in his old beat-up pick-up truck. Monica had an escalating drug problem that seemed to be getting worse as her boyfriend's absence continued.

There was little Tim could do about his girlfriend's problem. He was not financially independent and was still living with his mother. Tim just turned 18 in May, shortly after the families move to Colorado. Monica would not turn 18 until that November. Her problems just had to be put on a back burner, Tim reasoned, because he had to be more solvent financially before he could help her out.

With the opportunities now available to him, young Tim decided to put his nose to the proverbial grindstone and look for ways to make money. He went to Maxim Talent Agency in Denver to see if he could get work as a model or actor with them. After getting some head shots done, he would eventually be signed with Maxim as talent.

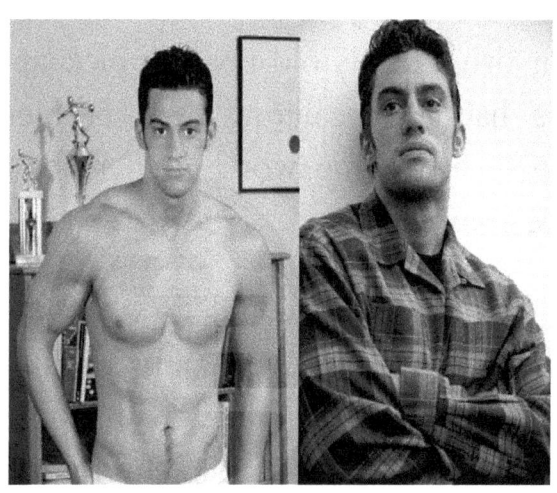

He immediately started getting work. He appeared in fashion shows, modeling various pieces of clothing. He also did photo shoots for catalog work for various companies like Sears. Monica would graduate from high school in May of 1998. She would regularly visit Tim in Denver and tried to entertain herself in between Tim's modeling gigs. Monica and Tim partied hard during this time, with her drug addiction becoming out of her control. Her drug of choice was cocaine. By early 2000 Monica was constantly back and forth between Stuart, Nebraska and Denver.

She was spending time with her boyfriend Tim Boham, and doing drugs, and wandering through life aimlessly. Sometime in the year 2000 Monica discovered she was pregnant. Tim and Monica were going to become teen parents. The mother of Monica was beside herself at the realization that her worst fear for her daughter had indeed become a reality. Now things were really going to change for young Timothy John Boham!

Chapter 4

Taking Care of Business!

For Tim's deeply religious mother Susan, she was dealing with mixed emotions regarding Monica's pregnancy. On one hand, she was relieved that neither her son nor Monica wanted to terminate the pregnancy. Yet Susan was concerned about the unborn child's future. Susan knew her son, whom she called 'John', was prone to fits of rage similar to his late father's. She was also fearful of Tim and Monica's future status as a couple. What kind of life was in store for this child, her future grandchild?

Monica was desperately trying to remain clean and sober during her pregnancy. It was very tempting for her to use. However for the sake of her baby girl, she did control her urges and stayed sober.

Tim, feeling very overwhelmed as the impending birth of his daughter, was struggling for solutions and plans to his unexpected predicament. Although Tim was getting modeling jobs through the agency, the money though was less than stellar. He had been saving his earnings for his own apartment in Denver. He was just about to turn 19, and he desperately wanted to live on his own, and relish his adulthood. He was starting to feel very stifled by his current living situation. He was living with his mom, stepfather and older sister Kate who at 21 was also still living at home.

Tim was about to be a father and realized he needed to start thinking about the future. Although he was overwhelmed and frightened, he was extremely excited about being a father. He was also very much in love with his girlfriend Monica and was very happy knowing he, Monica and their baby daughter would be together and be a family. He had always dreamed of one day having a large family. He would tell me, "I always wanted a really large family. With the white picket fence, the pretty wife, lots of cute healthy children."

Only time would tell if that was in the cards for young Tim Boham.

Tim had serious decisions to make regarding his future. His girlfriend Monica was pregnant, about to deliver in three months. She was making a serious attempt to remain drug free during her pregnancy. Tim was living at home, as he was signed talent with Maximum Talent in Denver. Like it or not, he accepted every job he was offered through them. He was desperately trying to put money together for an apartment. He wasn't sure about his future with Monica, but he knew there was a child coming that he had to help support.

Monica gave birth to a healthy baby girl that she named Jasmine. Tim went to the hospital in Nebraska shortly after the birth of his daughter. He was feeling a range of emotions. He was overjoyed at this new little life that he had a hand in creating. He was so proud of his beautiful little baby who looked a lot like her mother. Monica, on the other hand, seemed very depressed, so much so that Tim spoke with the doctor assigned to Monica at the hospital. The doctor assured Tim that this type of down feeling after the birth of a baby was quite normal for mothers to experience. He went on to say many mothers experience postpartum depression.

Shortly after Jasmine was born, the rest of Tim's family in Colorado made the trek to Nebraska to visit their new family member. They were all delighted and excited for Tim. He was now a father at 19, and they all pledged their support in helping him in any way they could.

Monica's mother had a lot on her plate. She was raising her two younger children, the oldest only eleven. She had to work two jobs just to make ends meet. As she told Tim and Monica on numerous occasions she was jut "plain exhausted." She could not at this time take on the care of a newborn. She felt she made that issue abundantly clear prior to Jasmine's birth. She actually pleaded with Monica before she left the hospital to please consider adoption. Monica ran the thought by Tim, who was vehemently opposed to the mere thought of it.

As he would recall years later, he thought, "Between myself, Monica, Mom and Kate we could make it work." He saw no reason to give up his own flesh and blood. He said once he saw her, once he saw his little beautiful daughter, he knew he could never consider such a thing. With adoption out of the question and Monica's depression growing worse by the hour, Tim was getting really anxious.

Monica and the baby were released from the hospital with Monica feeling extremely overwhelmed and out of sorts. She quickly started using again. It didn't take long for her to fall back into her old habits, as far as drugs and starting to hang around the wrong people.

Her mother tried in vain to remind Monica that she was now a mother, and she had to stop partying and get a job and support her baby. Tim was sending checks from Denver, but Monica was using, and the baby was quickly being neglected by Monica. The mother, and Jasmine's maternal grand-mother, had to step in and help with the infant's care. She was not pleased in the least that her fears were coming true.

Tim would recall years later, "I was overwhelmed every second. I was a new father at 19, I may as well been 39. I suddenly felt so old, it all felt so hopeless. I knew Monica was using, and I knew that things had to change very fast." Monica was starting to be gone for long periods of time, and her mother would constantly call Tim to come to Nebraska and take Jasmine so she could work. He would make the journey from Denver to Stuart, and decided to keep Jasmine with him in Colorado. He couldn't work and make the drive it was just too much.

His family tried their best to help the young overwhelmed father with Jasmine's overall care, but all of them—Susan, Kate and Walter—held down full-time jobs, so their time was very limited.

Boham apartment

Tim was in too deep. When Jasmine was only four months old, Monica was suddenly dead at the age of 19, from a suspected drug overdose. The circumstances of Monica's death were never really made clear, but her death was very tragic for all those involved. Now Jasmine would never know her mother, and Tim—at 19—was totally ill equipped to handle the demands of full time parenthood of an infant, it was a lot for anyone, let alone a teenager.

He started to marshal the proverbial forces after a very short time of grieving for his high school love that now was basically never meant to be. He was melancholy, many would observe, about her death. Some family felt that young Tim was sad that she died, but perhaps a bit relieved that the torment that consumed her was now over. He had mixed feelings over the effect her loss would be upon his young daughter. He reasoned that the child would have no memories of her mother, and therefore no knowledge of her constant struggles with drugs.

He thought it could actually be a new beginning for both himself and his daughter. Money however was still a constant struggle. All he knew was that he needed a lot more of it to support himself and Jasmine. He took his modeling to a new level in order to make more money and thus begin his descent into another world. A world a young man from the farm belt was completely unprepared for.

Chapter 5

From Modeling to Porn

Jasmine lost her mother when she was only six months old; her father, Tim Boham, was just nineteen. He had a chat with Monica's mother after the dust settled a bit, and he felt it was the right time. Monica's mom made it very clear that, as sad and tragic as it all was, she just could not take on the responsibility of the baby. She said she would support any decision Tim made regarding his daughter's future. She advised Tim to really think about adoption. She said Jasmine had a right to have the best chances for the best future, and with a nineteen-year-old father in charge, her chances of much of a future were very slim.

Tim didn't want to hear that, he was positive he could be a great parent. He knew it would be a struggle but, in his mind, he had no other options. He had to care for his daughter, and give her a "great life." He was – in a word – overwhelmed. He knew he had to make more money if he was going to raise his daughter. His family helped him while he worked and looked for other opportunities.

However, he sensed that they were all feeling the strain of caring for an infant. The work he was getting through Maximum Talent was not enough to support both of them. He rented a small, tiny room in the Capitol Hill area of Denver for himself and Jasmine, but life was a real struggle. His modeling started to morph into other areas! He started working at clubs in Denver as a male dancer, which lead to other work for a Denver-based company called "Boys Next Door."

It was basically an escort service, catering to married men, mostly middle-aged married men that were living on the 'down low'. Meaning during the day, they played it straight, with the wife, children, house, friends, barbecues, etc. When no one was looking, these same men would scour the ads of 'Backpage' and 'Craigslist' looking for young men aged 21 to 30 mostly. Tim would recall he started to get regular clients, same guys every week would call him for 'sessions'.

Asked what a session entailed, he merely shrugged his shoulders and said, "Whatever they wanted." He went on to say, "I was so far down that it didn't matter, whatever they asked for, they got, and I got money to pay the bills, and it was just about that, surviving."

Tim may well have thought he was 'far down' at that point, he would eventually realize that 'Far Down' was a lot lower than the men that contacted him through 'Backpage' and 'Craigslist'. It was about making money and taking care of his daughter's needs. He said he loved his little girl and just wanted to make her life "joyful". He was asked point blank how he could have possibly thought that being a male escort was the only road to take to provide for his daughter. Was he proud of the decision? He responded, "No, in hindsight, it was a horrible decision, but I was desperate, I had to support her, she only had me, and I had to do what I had to do." Tim said that he most certainly would not have made those dark choices had he not been a young single father. There is no way to know if that is indeed true, because that is what he did chose to do, and no one has the ability to go back and erase the past and change it. So we are all left to wonder.

Tim, through these contacts he was meeting, was convinced that if there was ever a hope of getting out of the escort business in Denver, he had to broaden his proverbial horizons. He was sure going to cities like New York or L.A. was his way out of that life. He had no idea how he was going to get out of the male escort business, but he decided that more opportunities would be available to him elsewhere. Therefore he made temporary arrangements for Jasmine to be taken care of by family and friends, and headed west to LA. He set out for the City of Angels in the spring of 2002, staying at a few seedy motels in Hollywood. He got himself a trade paper, and went about the grind of attending the various casting calls, sometimes known as 'cattle calls'. He said if he saw any type of part, print or film or stage that remotely resembled his type he was there. Going to these casting calls was an exhausting grind according to Tim. He would drive all over the greater L.A. basin, sometimes facing hours of traffic, to get there and just be a random face in a sea of like types of 20-somethings from all over the country—and sometimes other countries—looking for that lucky break.

However, like many aspiring models and actors before him, he quickly learned the task of 'making it in Hollywood' would be a rather daunting task. He gave himself a six-month deadline of getting a real part in something, anything, before he would just 'pack it all in'. While he was in Los Angeles, he had to survive, and he had to send money back to Denver for the care of Jasmine. He picked up side jobs while there: he parked cars for special events, picked up day jobs, and did what he had to do to get by. He signed with an agency that got aspiring actors extra work. Also he did do a bit of

Intended for Mature Audiences/Donna Thomas

extra work in the film industry, mostly just making scale wages! He said it amounted to about a $180.00 for a ten-hour work day. Some may have considered themselves lucky to be getting the $180 a day, but Tim thought he could and should be doing a lot better than that.

Prostitution is alive and well in the 'City of Angels', it's no great secret that 'women of the night' normally troll the streets of Hollywood—namely on Sunset Boulevard—looking for potential customers. There is a well-known area of the city that men do the same. It's in West Hollywood, on Santa Monica Boulevard.

I directly asked Tim if he was walking the streets of Santa Monica Boulevard looking for 'johns' while he was waiting for his lucky break. He said "I can't recall now, but I did what I had to do to survive, and take care of my daughter." That pretty much answered the questions as far as I was concerned.

Exactly two days before Tim's self-imposed six-month deadline, Tim was walking down

Santa Monica Boulevard on his way back to the room he had rented, when he crossed paths with a man, who did a double take, when he saw the young aspiring model/actor! The man turned around and shouted back to Tim, "Hey, are you an actor?". It almost sounds like a line from a Hollywood script, however, according to Tim, that is what happened. Tim turned around to see a short man with glasses standing there, looking at him. He said, "Are you talking to me?"

The man said, "Well, because of your look, I just thought maybe you were an actor." Tim told the man he was going on auditions, and trying to get work. The man gave him a business card, and said, "Call me, I make movies, and I have a lot of work; you can make a lot of money."

Tim looked down at the card, the name read 'Chi Chi LaRue'. It was the name of a person that would irrevocably change Tim's life forever. Tim looked down at the card, and said 'What kind of movies do you make?'".

Chi Chi told Tim, he made adult films. Tim asked what kind of adult films he made. Chi Chi said, he made porno films.

Tim thanked the man, who told him that he had to get to an appointment, but he would expect a call from him. The man, according to Tim, was very cordial to him, and said that he should call him and they could get together and have dinner, and discuss possibilities. Tim put the man's card in his pocket, and says he didn't give it a huge amount of thought on his way back to his room.

A call to Tim's mother later that day revealed all kinds of needs that his young daughter Jasmine had. Tim was starting to get anxious, and was deciding on whether he should prepare to go back to Denver or stay in LA for a few more days. Things were starting to weigh very heavy on his mind. He knew that he had a few more days left before he was going to have to go back to Denver. It wasn't just the self-imposed date. He had a young daughter back in Denver that was being cared for by others. He couldn't just continue to stay longer in LA on a whim. He was not young and carefree anymore, he was a young single father. He had to keep in close contact with his family, as to when he would be returning. He knew he either had to start making money in L.A. or he would have to return to Denver and starting looking for a full-time job. He had aspired to be an actor from the time he was a very young boy growing up in central Nebraska. He believed he had enough talent and drive to see his dreams materialize. He tried to put out some calls in Denver while he was still in L.A., trying to figure out if he could get any kind of decent full-time job while in Denver. The job market was tight in Denver around 2005. He felt that even though things were not yet happening in L.A. for him career wise, they could at any time. He thought going back to Denver would permanently shatter his dreams of stardom completely.

However, he knew he had to make a sound decision quickly, he said he felt like entire world was resting right on his shoulders. Tossing around those thoughts in his mind made him feel extremely anxious. He knew the clock was ticking and time was running out. He pulled that man's card out of his pocket and looked at it. He thought that he really should call that man, and at the very least listen to what he had to say before he headed back to Denver. With that thought in his mind, he dialed the number on the card, and was met with an answering machine. He left the man a message, and let him know he was the guy he had met earlier in the day on Santa Monica Boulevard and he would really like to talk to him.

Chi Chi LaRue called Tim back later that day, and the two spoke. It was at the end of that phone call that Tim decided to meet Chi Chi LaRue again the next day! There really was no turning back now. Later Tim recalled that when he called Chi Chi, he knew his life would be different after that. How or why, he couldn't explain but he just knew, and it would from this point forward never again resemble the life he was now living.

It wasn't likely Tim did any type of research on the types of films Chi Chi made before he called him. He recalled, "I was hungry, I know people use that word a lot, but I was literally starving to death. My mom complaining about me being gone so long. It was hard on her and the rest of family. Me being gone and them having to take care of Jasmine was tough on everyone. I'm not blaming anyone but myself. I felt really pressured to make something happen so, at the very least, I didn't have to go back as a total failure. So, no, I didn't check Chi Chi out before I called him. But in all honesty if I had, and found out exactly what he done, I can't say now after the fact, if that would have made any difference. Probably not, since I was desperate for money. Not just for me, but for my daughter, I had to do what I had to do, I felt she would understand in the end. I didn't imagine she would ever find out either. You never think about long range consequences – or I didn't, anyway. So the answer, nah, I didn't check him out, I guess I didn't want to know all the details."

The bottom line here is Tim didn't check into the types of films Chi Chi made prior to calling him. If he had, would the end result be different, as far as what transpired? It's anyone's guess, but Tim didn't check, he just moved forward, with the thought of making some money, and doing what he had to do. He was on a collision course that only time could determine the outcome.

Chapter six

Falcon Films ~ Chi Chi LaRue

The chance meeting that Tim Boham had with Chi Chi on Santa Monica Boulevard would have irrevocable consequences. For Chi Chi LaRue was a major player in the adult film industry. He was so known as a major player for a variety of reasons. Chi Chi LaRue was born Larry David Paciotti and grew up Pennsylvania in – by his own admission – a very staid traditional type of household.

As of this writing Chi Chi is 54 years old, and identifies himself as a gay man. When I became acquainted with Tim Boham at the Denver County jail on Smith Rd, we had many conversations regarding Chi Chi. For even I had heard of Chi Chi prior to my first meeting with Tim. Chi Chi moved to Minnesota from Pennsylvania, and after the move, started to perform in drag shows as the female character 'Chi Chi LaRue'. He appeared in full drag, wigs, make-up, clothing, high heels etc with another drag performer. They were billed as the "Weather Girls".

***

Paciotti – or 'Chi Chi' – became acquainted with many adult film performers and drag performers in the Minneapolis – Saint Paul area. It was through these various associations, Chi Chi decided to move to Los Angeles. He felt that he could go further in the adult film industry, in which he developed an acute interest. His interest was in the capacity of a director. He wanted to direct adult films; he had started to dabble in the art on a very amateurish level in Minneapolis. He took to the role of director very easily, and started to excel in the role, and felt that he was ready to really purse the art aggressively, so that he could prosper in the field. He knew that Los Angeles was the quote end quote "Porno Capitol of the world," He unequivocally knew L.A. was where he had to be.

***

When Chi Chi pulled up stakes to L.A, he started to make gains rather quickly in the porno world. His first job of note, upon his move to the City of Angels, was with 'Catalina Films', as an administrative assistant. He was known by his stage name 'Chi Chi LaRue' in almost all of his business dealings. He started to move very quickly up the ranks of the porno world, making very impressive films and splitting his time between different adult film companies. His first credited film in a directorial position was made in 1988. As of this writing, Chi Chi has directed over one thousand gay, straight and bi pornographic films.

Not only is Chi Chi a director, but he acts as a producer, and owns his own production companies. Of note they are *Channel One, Rascal*

Films, and probably the most well-known pornographic film company in the world *Falcon Films*. Some of the most well-known pornographic actors in the world have worked under this label, including Jenna Jamison, who is a close friend of Chi Chi's.

He had extensive directing credits while he was at *Vivid Films*, which now produces a large number of 'celebrity' sex tapes, including those made by reality starts, Kim Kardashian, Paris Hilton and Farrah Abraham.

He had a very well-known falling out with *Vivid Films* in 2006. The last known film that he directed under the Vivid label was made in 2005. The reason that Chi Chi claimed he left Vivid was their refusal to insist the actors they used wore condoms. He said that he could no longer be involved with a film company that didn't promote the safest and highest industry standards for insuring safe sex on the set.

Chi Chi, in many interviews in print and film, has consistently called himself the "Condom

Nazi." In some quarters the magazine, 'Out Magazine', is known as a proverbial bible in the LGBT community. In 2007 Chi Chi was named by the magazine in the annual list of the fifty most influential people in the LGBT community.

He has won several awards in the porn industry from 1990 to 2013. Some of the awards include best director, best video, best film. Many of the awards were handed down by AVN which is acronym for Adult Video News, an organization which generally sets the industry standards.

Chi Chi has been attributed to more than his fair share of controversies. He is highly credited as the person that first used the term "Straight For Pay," meaning a gay actor will perform in pornographic film in a straight scene solely for money. He famously directed the adult film actor, Blake Riley, in his first pornographic film opposite a woman. It was said to be Riley's first ever sexual encounter with a woman. Riley was discovered by LaRue, and had until this 2007 film only appeared in gay pornographic films. The film was titled 'Shifting Gears' and upon its 2007 release generated a lot of controversy.

Chi Chi has also been involved in the producing and directing of many music videos. He has made numerous claims of having a zero tolerance for unsafe medical practices on his many film sets. One of the reasons that Tim specifically mentioned as his reasons for leaving the porn industry was his fear of contracting a deadly diseases like HIV and/or AIDS.

When pressed on the issue, Tim directly told me – during our many chats at the Denver County jail – that actors on sets were "visibly sick." I asked him what he meant by visible sick. He said, "People had legions on their skin, dark purple and blue legions." He went on to elaborate that, "The sick look, and weak and tired, was always the pink elephant in the room."

I had been doing my research before every meeting I had with Tim, so that I had lots of material to discuss with him.

One of the big things I uncovered was Chi Chi's constant remarks regarding his insistence that condoms be used on all of his sets. What Tim told me regarding this issue alone was in direct contrast to what Chi Chi was known for. Tim said, "All these actors were sick; and if they weren't yet sick, they were on their way to being sick." By the word 'sick' I could determine that Tim was referring to AIDS or HIV. When he talked in these terms he meant that the actors he was working with in films had AIDS or HIV. He said Chi Chi had to have seen it; if he (Tim) saw it so did Chi Chi. Tim added, "He knew they were all sick, he didn't care, he wanted what he wanted, even if these people infected everyone, He just didn't give a shit."

I was very surprised by this, not because I found it shocking, but only because Chi Chi made such a big public point of saying he demanded condoms be used on his sets. He also said that he insisted that all his actors be health checked regularly. Tim said he didn't once have to be health checked and he doubted very seriously that these people with purple legions were health checked either.

Chapter seven

Retirement at 23

Tim's work in the Adult film industry was new and very exciting at first. If he had any apprehension about performing, whatever that was, it would eventually fade away. According to Tim post porn, it very scary at first. He explained his first day on an adult film set during an interview with me in a little tiny jail cell at the Denver County Jail on Smith Road. He would tell me, "I knew what I had to do before I got there, but knowing and doing are two different things." He went on to describe what he felt when he did a porno movie for the first time. It was unreal.

One of his early films released in 2003, was titled "Bedtime Stories" produced by, *Studio 2000*. Tim was beginning to tell me his high tales of his freshman porno year. He said he only had about an hour to come up with a stage name, he threw out many names, but none were well received. He thought of Marcus Allen the football player. He said he thought, "He did it like I want to do, get out there, play your best game, and reach retirement." Tim would say, "That's what I wanted to do, go in and make a lot of money and get out."

The large majority of the porn films that Tim appeared in were categorized as gay porn. Tim would be filmed in various scenes having sex with other men. His earlier modeling career in Denver had morphed into a stint as a male escort, getting customers through primarily "Boys Next Door." Tim explained all about the porn industry to me as we sat in that tiny visiting room at the Denver County Jail. He said, "It's hard to imagine what it feels like. You walk into a room that is already set up; most of these films were shot in the Valley".

Tim was referring to the San Fernando Valley, right outside of Los Angeles, and still Los Angeles County. "The most number of porn films in the world are produced in the Valley, over ninety percent," Tim went on to explain. "There you are with your partner or partners, performing these scenes, and all the sex acts are staged; nothing is spontaneous, you're going completely off of a script. Every part of your body placement is staged and calculated before filming begins. There are people standing around the set: camera guys, stage people, script people, makeup people, it's got to be at least 30 people at any given time standing around, watching you have sex. It's very hard, eventually you just get numb, you kind of have to, or you can't really do it." He revealed that it came to a point that he could not film scenes without using alcohol and or drugs. He also revealed, "The first time I filmed a scene, I was awful. It had to be re-shot I don't even know how many times. I just kept thinking, someone I care about could see this one day, someone I know, could say there is John, he's just such trash, look what he's doing."

"When that was in my space, in my head, I just couldn't perform, I just went numb, I couldn't concentrate. The director finally said, 'Hey, just go over there and have a drink and loosen up. Do something, we're losing a lot of money here'. You know, I wish I would have just booked out of there and left. That was some kind of sign for me to just get the fuck out of there. All the telltale signs were there, but I was so desperate for money. I just made myself do it, and after I started doing it, it became a routine, like going to the gym."

I just had to ask him why he continued to do it if it was that miserable; why didn't he leave. He was young, nice looking, very polite; this was the only job he could find, in the entire city of fourteen million people, a porno performer? The end all be all so to speak, he couldn't find some other job that could support himself and his young daughter? I just couldn't image that this healthy young guy, strong and very smart, white, no criminal record at that point, couldn't do anything else. I asked that question directly.

His answer was honest in my opinion, "I probably could have, but, you know, I had been an escort when I needed money and it was good money. The porn shit was a lot better money then the escorting. I just couldn't go take a job for little to nothing an hour with a young kid to feed. I was used to making decent money as a model and an escort, I couldn't, I thought at that point, go work construction or retail or at a food place, it wouldn't have been enough money to pay the bills. That sounds like an excuse even now as I'm saying it, but that's the reality of what I thought at that moment."

I just sat there and listened to him, and didn't say much.

***

"So what was Chi Chi LuRue like to work with?" I had asked him.

He said "I didn't even know who he was when I first saw him, I just thought he was some drag queen that directs porno flicks, Had no idea about the type of legend in the porno industry overnight that he was, when I first met him,. I had never really paid attention to the porn industry and especially not gay porn. So how would I have known about him?"

Tim started to climb the ladder of success in the proverbial ranks of the porn industry very fast, and accumulated a huge fan base the world over. He literally became very well known within the gay adult film industry. Some of the most standout films of his adult film career were, 'Never Been Touched', 'Body to Die For', 'Ripe', 'Road To Temptation', 'Through The Woods', 'Dirty Young Bucks' and 'A little Big League', to name just a few.

***

'Marcus Allen' didn't have a long, storied porn career, but he made a huge splash on the gay adult film industry in a relatively short amount of time. The majority of his films that garnered the most attention for him were produced and released between 2003 and 2005.

He racked up several awards from his colleagues in the industry. Among these were the covers of leading film industry magazines. He appeared on the cover of the hugely popular industry magazine, "Freshman Magazine" in November of 2002. He appeared in photo spreads for this magazine more than a dozen times, and also appeared on the cover of the porn magazine 'Mandate'.

He went to industry parties, and was the '*IT*" man, the guy that everyone wanted to be around.

Intended for Mature Audiences/Donna Thomas

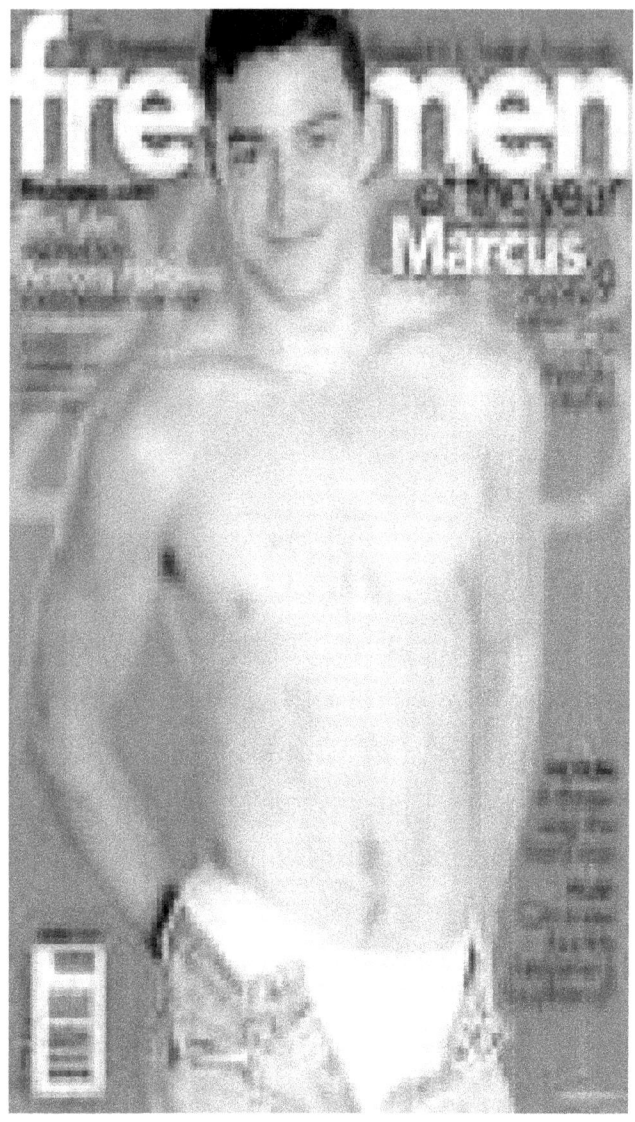

Some of the spoils of his new found 'fame' brought him new toys to play with. He bought a brand-new pick-up truck, after years of driving around in 'beaters'. He also was able to buy a new wardrobe and a custom-made Harley. Life was good on the outside according to Tim. He was doing what Chi Chi LaRue had coined "Gay For Pay." What Chi Chi had intended when he first threw out that term was that a lot of people that are not necessarily gay, could become that way if the price is right. Tim, who had a young child when he first walked onto the set of an adult film, never identified himself as gay. However, as the time went by, that's how his fans all over the world saw him. He knew that and he didn't like that little factoid very much.

For one thing, Tim Boham was leading a double life. No one outside of the adult film industry knew he made films. His family did not know, he would go to L.A. every few weeks or so to make a movie and go back to Denver to play single father. His family did not know, nor did his friends know that their friend John from Nebraska was one of the most well-known gay porno stars in the world. His family just thought he was going out to L.A. to do some modeling assignments, and audition for acting roles. He at some point would have to say he got some parts. How else could he have explained his ability to fly back and forth and more importantly support himself and his daughter? He had told his mother a few times, "Yeah, I'm not sure when it will be out, but it should be pretty good." He said he had to tell his mother Susan that more than a few times. If she was suspicious of what Tim was really doing in L.A., she never mentioned it to him or anyone else. He related to me that he lived in conflict with the morals and values he was raised with, and the facts of his current situation. Voila

As time went on, Tim was drinking more alcohol and using more drugs, to just get by. As he puts it just, "To make myself numb." He also said that working with Chi Chi LaRue was starting to "Become a real drag". It was just one thing after another with him. He went on to say, "I worked everyday under this horrible feeling that I would catch AIDS."

I asked him whatever would make him say that.

He said, "Everyone came to the set visibly sick."

I asked him what he meant by sick, he said, "Just sick with AIDS and shit." He described men coming to set with deep purple legions on their face and arms. He said Chi Chi saw it too, he must have. Tim had said the same thing earlier.

I told him that I heard that Chi Chi bills herself as a 'condom Nazi'. "Is that what he just threw out there, to sound politically correct," I asked.

He questioned, "What do you mean?"

I explained to him, "Chi Chi publicly says that he enforces safe sex on all his film sets."

"Not true," said Tim Boham. "He didn't care about any of that, he just cared that whatever diseases they had couldn't be seen through the camera lens. He's a big fat fraud." Tim said again, sometime after the killing.

Tim was becoming less and less cooperative with Chi Chi, and he began showing up late to his sets. He was heard saying anti-gay slurs under his breath. Actors started to complain to Chi Chi, they didn't want to work with Tim anymore because they viewed him as unstable, irrational, hard to work with. Some actually went so far as to say that Tim was a bully.

After his arrest, this issue would come back to haunt him for a time. I actually asked him about it, if all of these stories were true, did he ever say anti gay statements on set. He said, "Absolutely not!"

I challenged that response as too many different people were making the same allegations.

However Tim was defiant in his denials. He said, "If I hated gay people that much, why would I be making gay porno films?"

I said he made the films for money, and he was like Chi Chi said he was: "Gay For Pay."

"No, not true," said Tim, who was sitting in a jail cell, awaiting some very serious charges. Tim basically said that the porn industry just has a way of wearing you down little by little. He claimed that, one way or the other, "It rips away at your soul."

Pretty big words, from such a scared and frightened young man. I asked him "Is that why you're here (jail) because you were a porn star?"

He looked directly at me and said, "Well, it didn't help, and it's not going to help going forward."

***

Back in Los Angeles, Tim was just dreading going to the sets. He said his biggest fear was catching something deadly, like John Holmes. He referenced the late legendary porn star John Holmes also known as "Johnny Wadd", for his extremely large penis, who died in 1988 of AIDS. Tim was only seven years old when Holmes died.

I said, "Hey, I'm impressed. Holmes was before your time."

He said, "Yeah, but some guy took me by the last place he lived at in L.A., and then the guy dies broke of AIDS in a VA hospital. He was such a huge star, and then he's dead like that. In that way. I – for some reason – saw myself in him. I can tell you this, I really didn't like what I saw, and it scared the shit out of me."

Tim was showing up less and less, and Chi Chi was canceling gigs and shoots, and becoming one angry gay porn director, who was probably wishing he never laid eyes on young Timothy J. Boham.

***

Tim was starting to have serious issues with his young daughter and her care, and his ability to parent. He was leaving her not only with his family but with anyone else that would watch her, and that sometimes was not the best person. There are widely varying stories as to what the chain of custody was of young Jasmine Boham. His sister Kate and mother Susan were becoming unwilling or unable to care for the child when her father was out of town. That posed huge problems for Tim. The man who first encouraged Tim to be a male escort in Denver was becoming an element in the equation regarding his young daughter. The man, who I shall call Robert, would volunteer to watch Jasmine when Tim's family couldn't or wouldn't. Tim's sister Kate, had a serious car accident a few years earlier, she received serious injuries to her brain and back. She did suffer some brain damage, her recovery was a very slow and arduous process, fraught with pain and misery and severe depression. Tim's mother was dealing with a terminally ill father, and her own physical problems which included severe debilitating back pain. As time wore on, the stress of all these medical problems for Susan and Kate proved to be a horrendous obstacle affecting their availability or willingness to care for the tiny Boham.

Robert, knowing that Tim needed his help so he could go off and film his porno movies in L.A., was all too willing to watch Jasmine. Some may say that Tim should have been relieved to have found someone to help him with his daycare problems. However Tim was highly suspicious of Robert's kindness when it came to his daughter.

I asked Tim later in the interview why he was so hesitant and apprehensive of Robert's intentions.

Tim said, "Well, Robert was the one to get me into the escort business, knowing I had a baby I was trying to raise. I'm not blaming him for all the decisions I made, but he was a real sleazy guy, did anything for money, no morals, none. Yeah, I know I'm one that shouldn't be talking, but Jasmine is my daughter. you kind of have to love your family unconditionally. This Robert guy had no morals, and Jasmine wasn't his kid, but yet he always wanted to help me out. I just didn't think he was the person that Jasmine should have been left with."

These problems he was having with his daughter's care were weighing very heavily on his mind as his professional behavior was becoming more and more erratic. As he was rushing to get ready to go to the set of his then current movie in the Valley, he stopped in the bathroom to shave before he left. He recalled, "I don't know what clicked or what happened exactly but I was standing there shaving looking at myself in the mirror. I just said, 'You are such a loser, you should be doing so much more with yourself. What about if Jasmine finds out, what about if she knows, she would be so ashamed of her own father'? I just couldn't take it another day, I thought any job, anywhere would be so much better than this. I finished shaving, and thought, *Fuck it, I can't go anymore, not doing it. Whatever happens, happens, but this life has to be done with.*"

He packed what he could get in his truck, and then and there got into his vehicle and drove East to Denver. No call to the set, no long drawn out goodbyes with anyone, just stone-cold silence. He left his little attachment to the porn industry that made him a 'Star'. He left L.A. and began the long thousand-mile plus drive back to Denver, and – according to him – never looked back, not even once.

'Marcus Allen' was no more as of that day.

Chapter eight

J(ohn). P(aul). Kelso

John Paul Kelso! Oh boy, where to begin? I guess I will start with my own personal interactions with J.P. as most people that knew him called him. J.P. owned a collection agency in Denver, Colorado called Professional Recovery Services, aka PRS. It was a very large office on the 24th floor of a building right in the heart of downtown Denver. It employed at any given time twenty-five full-time bill collectors. J.P. amassed a small fortune in the credit and collection industry. His forte was buying written-off debt for pennies on the dollar. In other words, debt that companies pr creditors deemed to be not collectable. J.P. owned the debt outright. So there was no third party involved with any of the debt he bought for his agency; he owned it. Which is a bit of a different spin then most other like agencies employed. Most others would acquire clients, like let's say SEARS and call delinquent accounts, AKA as debtors, and whatever amounts were collected would be split by the collection agency and the client the debt belongs to. The percentage the collection agency gets is negotiated in the contract between the agency and the client.

Typically the amounts are about forty percent of the collected debt. So say for example, the agency collects a hundred dollars, they keep forty and return sixty to the client. There can be a huge variance of these fees, depending on individual negotiations. However in the case of the debt acquired by J.P, he bought it for literally pennies on the dollar, and anything anyone collected was basically all profit. Nice little niche if you can perfect it.

I was looking for some extra income, so I inquired of several agencies to see if anyone needed a good skip tracer, or someone that can assess assets for possible suits. I have had extensive experience doing both. Someone from PRS called and scheduled an interview with me.

I made my way to my appointment and was interviewed by the collection manager, Chad. I was hired as a skip tracer. My basic task was to locate debtors, by means commonly employed by agencies, checking different data banks for any information that would lead to the whereabouts of the debtor. I was assigned a very small desk in the very back of the collection floor. Most of the people working there on the collection floor were bill collectors. It was a very tense environment, and from the basic chatter that I could hear, was that most people who worked there were extremely unhappy and scouring the wants ads constantly. A few days would pass before I would actually encounter the owner of the establishment, Mr. J.P. Kelso.

Before I actually saw him, there was a rather thin young man with very dark hair that was always hovering about the executive offices, as they were called. I asked someone who that was, and the girl replied "Oh that's Seth, J.P.'s boyfriend."

I never was positive what exactly Seth did, he always looked busy doing nothing, but then again, Kelso had a lot of men around that didn't seem to be doing anything specific in particular.

He, (Seth) had a very scared, timid look about him. He couldn't have been more then 23 or 24. He was young, and some may have found him attractive. He was tall—maybe 6 feet. I didn't think anything of it, other than that the owner of this place is gay.

I saw J.P. one day stroll into an office where this Seth was sitting. He was short, fat and at least 20 years older than Seth. He was just a short, bloated man that kind of looked like a frog to me. Perhaps now looking back on my recollections of J.P, he was an ugly unattractive person, more so because of the way he treated people than the way he looked. He was not attractive by most people's standards, but kindness can overshadow most negative physical attributives.

Kind is not a word that would immediately come to my mind when thinking back on my recollections of J.P. Kelso. He regularly yelled at people in his employ, he berated them for under-performing or any and every other reason. Instead of him taking someone into an office and having a civilized discussion with that person, he yelled and ridiculed people in full view of the entire office. It was easily the most negative, toxic work environment I had ever had the unfortunate luck of being in. It was tense in there all the time, and people standing up, yelling, screaming. Walking out on the job was a regular occurrence. Although the wages at PRS were higher than other agencies, the work environment there generated an extremely high turn-over rate.

I only worked there part time, but it was enough to give me a full blown migraine headache one hundred percent of the time. I would come home from there, and regularly tell my husband Steve what a hostile work environment that place was. The extra income the part-time gig generated was very much needed, the ill effects of that work environment weren't.

Unbeknownst to me, Steve decided to show up at PRS for lunch one day.

However, just showing up was never Steve's style. He had a box of Kripsy Creme donuts and a white boat type of paper hat with the words 'Krispy Creme' on it, on his head. He arrived at the front desk of PRS, where he announced to Alice the secretary that he had arrived to "Take my wife to lunch." He said "I come bearing sugar to sweeten up this rather negative, sour environment."

Someone let me know, that I had a visitor at the front desk. I headed to the desk in the waiting area. As I was walking there, I saw J.P. come out of his office and head to that same desk. He asked Steve "What are you doing". Steve proceeded to tell him he was there to take me out to lunch. Kelso said "This is an office and we're in the middle of the work day, we don't have time for these types of games."

Steve said, "Well maybe you should make time. No one here seems to like you very much.

My wife tells me you yell at people in full view of the entire office. I told her that can't be so, no respectable decent human being would do such a thing. I had to come and see for myself."

I know Steve didn't need a formal introduction to J.P., I guess his physical appearance offered a clue that this little man my 6'4" husband was looking down on was the infamous J.P. Kelso.

Without missing a beat J.P replied to Steve, "Well, I'm not here to have anyone like me, I'm here to make money."

Steve told him, "You won? Lots of cash, no real friends."

That could seem harsh, but it was very hard to like J.P. Kelso, I didn't actually know anyone that did.

A good friend of mine I've mentioned previously, Tim Walkup – who at that time owned a collection agency in Denver called BRW Financial Group – had at different times done business with J.P. He knew him very well. He recalled for me after the fact the day that he had met J.P. He said he went up to his office, and when he walked through the office door to greet J.P, he extended him his hand. He said "J.P. took my hand and turned it around and looked at it very closely."

I asked Tim what he thought J.P. was looking at. Tim responded, "Who knows, but I thought it was very weird. I never had anyone ever do that before or after meeting him."

Another person named Frank that owns a collection agency in South Denver, also knew J.P. "Well, he told me, "J.P. is a decent enough guy, but he certainly has his personal demons." He recalled for me a time when he and a lot of other people were invited to one of J.P.'s legendary birthday parties. He said, "It was in Las Vegas, he openly introduced Seth to me as his boyfriend." Frank said he thought everyone knew that Seth was J.P.'s boyfriend.

I asked Frank if he was surprised when he learned J.P. had died. He said, "Not at all, he was a very troubled person."

J.P. had an older sister and mother, and had a very strained problematic relationship with both of them, and barley spoke to either of them. His family lived in Denver and other cities, but J.P. rarely saw them. He was gay, flashy and to all who knew him, a very heavy drinker, who was plagued with self esteem issues.

In addition to booze, J.P. was also into drugs. His drug of choice? Coke! Many different people have stories of J.P's drunken exploits. Perhaps the fact that J.P was openly gay caused a rift within his family. I'm not sure, I never really asked him about any of that, I didn't know him well, I had limited interactions with him. Most people were aware of the fact that his sister Kimberly Maclaren and mother Suzanne Kelso barely had a relationship with him.

The status of those relationships would be the subject of much discussion during his murderer's trial, but to my knowledge and according to Tim Walkup, he didn't really get along with his family members. I experienced a very unhealthy work environment at P.R.S. Although I needed the extra income, I decided that I would resign. The way J.P treated people and the outward hostility in the work place there, was just in my opinion not worth the heartache working there caused me.

I drafted my resignation letter. I basically told J.P. he was a horrible bastard who thought he was just on top of the world. "Nothing and no one can touch you." I wrote. "However." I said in my letter to him, "One day the King of the Island just may not have any islanders to rule over."

I was certain any advise I wished to share with that bullfrog would be totally lost on him. However I felt compelled to write to that son of a bitch. I came in and asked Alice if I could go in and see King Tut for a moment. I waited for what felt like an eternity. She said "You can go in now."

I went into his office and handed him my letter. I said, "J.P., you get more of these letters then Santa receives. I can no longer work for you, you're an insufferable bastard and I can't stand to look at your ugly face for another second." I got up from the chair I was sitting in, and headed for the door, and said, "I'll be getting the things out of my desk and leaving."

Not waiting for a response from him, I walked out of his office and headed to my desk, gathered my things very quickly, said a few goodbyes to the unfortunate folks that were still there in that horrible quagmire and headed out towards the exit door.

J.P. was standing in front of his office with a smug look on his face. He was such a horrible nasty little man, I was so glad to be getting out of there. His smile was unnerving to me. He said "Don't let the door hit you on the way out." Boy, he was original. He was such an asshole, no other word in my opinion could describe that worthless sphincter muscle. I could have, and maybe should have taken the high road as I was walking out of there to leave, but I just couldn't resist. After he said that snarky remark, I walked right up to him and said" You know, J.P., you're such a smug callous little piece of shit. You think you're so smart. One of these days, you're going to piss off the wrong person, for all it takes is one wrong person and then they will put one in you, and it will all be over."

He said, "Oh, yeah, Donna, whatever you say."

With that, I didn't answer him and just walked out, and I looked back as I was going to the elevator. He was standing there in front of the front desk with his arms folded in front of him, and he was smirking. All I could think about was what a smug bastard he was and how happy I was to leave that place. Exactly six years to the day, I gave him my parting words, he was dead with a bullet in his head. *Very eerie, is all I can say, very eerie indeed!*

It's quite interesting that after he died, so many people were saying what a nice man he was, and how kind he was. I couldn't believe they were talking about the same J.P. that I knew. I wondered how they could say that; were they romanticizing him in death? It had to be that—people have a tendency to do that. I can't bring myself to do likewise. No one should die the way he did, but I didn't like him in life, he was mean and nasty.

Most people that I knew who knew him did not like him either. I had never heard one person prior to his death say anything nice about J.P. Kelso. My husband Steve said, "The air in that office was so thick and so heavy, he was just a very toxic person." Steve was a very insightful man, and he knew, he basically told me that, "I get why you don't like him now, I totally get it."

***

I reached out to Seth Hill to see if he wanted to share anything about J.P. He testified at the trial. Basically, like he did at PRS, a whole lot of nothing. He didn't say he was J.P's lover on the stand, nor to me. Even so, Tim Walkup knew that Seth was J.P.'s lover. He has a lot of years of work experience at PRS on his Linked-in page. Frank also said that he knew that Seth was J.P.'s lover. He was terse belligerent and nasty to me, in the brief exchanges that we had. He closed with, "You don't have my permission to use my remarks or name in your tabloid."

Well, Seth I own my story, and you're now in it, and were in it when I first laid eyes on you back in the day. Please become one with intellectual property laws.

Perhaps his problem is with everyone and their mother knowing that he was J.P.'s little boy wonder, in more ways than one, and advanced in the business world for reasons other than his superior business mind and vast knowledge. In my opinion anyway! He really needs to calm way down.

***

J.P. Kelso had a long criminal record for forgery, theft, embezzlement and a host of other offenses. So much so that he couldn't have a business license for a collection agency in his name. So theoretically he didn't even own PRS. His 'business partner'—John Sawyer—was on the license. Did Mr. J.P. Kelso contribute much to the world? That's subject to interpretation. He made a lot of money, and made a lot of enemies along the way, and to his detriment, one deadly enemy!

Chapter nine

Murder in Congress Park

There are different versions of stories regarding how J.P. Kelso and Tim Boham met each other. There is Tim's version, the one he told me before the trial. There is the one he told on the witness stand. I believe the truth is closer to the version he told me before the trial. A lot of what he said on the stand was pure fabrication, cooked up to save his neck and hide from the electric chair. Colorado does have the death penalty, not implemented as often as in other states, but nevertheless it is used.

***

In the before trial version, Tim told me that after he left the porn industry permanently in 2005 and was living Denver full time, he was desperately looking for work. Tim recalled that he was sitting at a coffee shop on Colfax Avenue near the capital, and he was scouring the want ads in the Denver Post.

J.P. was in the coffee shop that morning also. The shop must have been only five minutes away from J.P.'s downtown office. As Tim was drinking coffee and circling ads, a "little fat man approached."

J.P. asked Tim if he was Marcus Allen by any chance.

Tim taken aback by the use of his porn name, said, "No, my name is John."

J.P. was defiant in his belief that Tim was indeed Marcus Allen. Tim assured the stranger standing over him that he was not this Marcus

Allen, his name really was John and he was busy.

J.P asked Tim if he was looking for a job.

Tim told J.P. that yes, he was in fact looking for work. He would consider any type of work.

J.P. said, "Great. I have a collection agency, and I'm always looking for good people."

"Well, I don't have any type of experience, doing that type of work." Tim told J.P..

J.P. told Tim that he should come down to the office and perhaps they could work something out. He gave Tim his business card, and told him to call him anytime.

Tim called him a few days later and he went over to PRS to talk to J.P about working there. When he got there he felt a tinge of ambivalence because he knew it wasn't the type of work environment he would thrive in. Not only would he not thrive in it, he thought right out of the gate, he wouldn't like it there. But he was there, and he needed a job, so he was going to listen to what J.P. had to say.

***

Tim was warmly embarrassed by J.P., like they were long-lost friends that just found each other, or they had known each other for years. Well, neither of those scenarios was the case. It was just J.P. over extending himself to a young good-looking guy that he wanted to have sex with. That was the modus operandi of J.P. Kelso. That's what he did his entire adult life. Most of the young men that were ever in his life were paid to be there.

As horrible as that sounds, that's the truth. I've heard people after his death say what a wonderful person he was. He was so kind, people said. He gave of his time and resources to help others, that's what some people said about him. The man was in his mid-forties when he was killed. He never had one serious relationship with any man that was his financial equal.

***

Of course there are many couples that are not equal in the financial arena; that of course can happen. However if in every single partner that is the case, there more than likely are issues. Could he not ever find a partner that loved him for him, and not his money?

I don't think so, not from what I personally saw of him, or from what I have learned from others or what I know now. Tim Boham was no different than all the others; he became involved with J.P. because J.P. had money and Tim didn't, and he wanted some of his money, it's really that simple.

Well, Tim decided to try working at PRS, because, frankly, other than going back to porn or being an escort again, there was nothing else on the horizon at the moment. He was new to the world of credit and collections, and being a bill collector is no easy feat. Some may think it is, but it's not, it takes a certain type of person to be able to do it, and do it well. Tim was a model and an escort, and a porn star; the absolute polar opposite of what a bill collector is. You have to be very accommodating and pleasing in the type of work Tim was used to doing.

In order to be a successful bill collector, you have to be authoritative, and menacing and in complete control at all times in order to collect money, and if you don't collect money you don't eat.

Tim reported to PRS the day after he met with J.P. to start training as a bill collector. His first day was spent sitting beside a seasoned bill collector named Jim who had been doing collections for over 20 years. Tim wore a headset so he could hear all the collection calls being made from the terminal he was sitting at. He later recalled he knew after the first five calls there was no way he could do it, but he tried to muster up any and all acting skills he had, and just make believe he was really happy to be there.

I guess his 'acting skills' failed him miserably during the first day. People that recounted their memories with Tim at PRS after the fact, all basically said the same thing. He seemed like he had other things on his mind, like he didn't really want to be there.

Well, Tim was a porn actor. They don't have enough lines to learn usually, so that may be part of the reason his acting skills were lacking. He finished out day one, and J.P. caught him as he was getting up to leave the office. They talked and J.P. wanted Tim to go out later that night, but Tim declined and said he would be back in the morning. Tim was back at PRS the next morning, he was still sitting with Jim listening to calls, and watching the computer monitor to see how files were notated.

After an hour of training, Tim was expected to at least start making collection calls. Tim tried his best and tried to make a few calls, but he found it to be extremely difficult. He said it just wasn't his thing, "It's kind of like a sales job. I just never really liked the sales thing."

So with that sentiment Tim was out of there, never to look back again after a grand total of almost two days. This was 2006. Tim was already looking to greener pastures. Interesting thing to me is that he looked at a debt collector job as a sales job. He didn't like the fact that it was 'like' a sales job. Don't you sell something when you're an escort? Isn't that all about sales? Maybe not, but I certainly thought escorting was all about sales, and nothing more. Learn something new every day, I suppose!

***

I couldn't really fault Tim for leaving PRS in the way he did. After all, after some thought I was gone, too. I tried a bit longer then he did, but in the end I was out of there. I couldn't get out of there fast enough. It was just a matter of time for most people that worked there. If it wasn't the job itself, it was the unbearable working conditions that one had to endure for that meager paycheck.

Tim has afterwards said publicly that he had a friendship with J.P. He claimed after the collection position went south, he and J.P tried to have a sexual relationship for money, but it didn't work out, so it simply reverted to a friendship. That isn't the truth. All anyone had to do was look at the two side by side to know that was a load of horse manure that Tim was trying to sell to save his butt. If he had a second of interaction with J.P. money was involved that second or in a future second. It is really that simple. Again it was all about money, and Tim's desire to get his hands on it.

Tim was a hustler that was constantly eying his next prey. J.P. – as bad as he was – was lonely, and hungered for the attention of young good-looking men. He would try to attain that attention with money and lavish gifts; anything and everything to win his cherished prizes, he would do without a second thought.

Tim said under oath that it was a mutual friend of his and J.P's named Dan that encouraged him to go to J.P.'s house and have sex with J.P. for money. That was for the public. Based on what Tim admitted before the trial, I don't think Tim needed any encouragement to screw someone for money, he had been doing it for years by the time he met J.P.

Tim had on a prior occasion enlisted into the National Guard. He never actually went to any type of basic training. He did take the Armed Services Vocational Battery exam, (ASVAB) and got the minimum score needed to enlist. He kept putting off actually going off to boot camp. After he was not able to hack the bill collector job at PRS he was kind of in limbo, as far as work and money.

He didn't dare care cut J.P. loose, for he knew the man was good for some quick easy cash. He started to drink heavily at this point, and started to go out and party. He went out to a bar in Denver one night solo and sat at the bar. The bartender that night was a pretty 23-year-old named Christina Hernandez, who was originally from San Diego. He said he was instantly attracted to her, and he sat at the bar until it closed down, sometime after 2 a.m. He gave Christina his number, and in just a few weeks he referred to Christina as his girlfriend.

At this time, Tim really needed a place to stay, and fearing he would ruin things with Christina, he asked J.P. if he could stay with him for a short time. That was the summer of 2006. He went back to a recruiter to see if he could still enlist in the National Guard, he was told he could so he reenlisted, even though he was never really in to begin with.

He didn't stay with J.P. more than a few weeks. The plan was for Tim to actually go to boot camp this time. He stayed in a bedroom on the east side of the home, and there is only Tim's word at the trial to verify that. He then stayed with a friend of his named Denny that lived in West Denver after he left J.P.'s house. He was getting back into escorting at this time, because, well, it seemed that nothing in the "straight world" was really panning out for him.

He would go out to L.A. to do his escorting for an agency named 'Meet The Stars'. A man named David Forrest owns it. Forrest is the middle man that arranges 'dates' between high profile porn stars and male clients.

I talked to David Forest about his dealings with Tim. He is a convicted felon that spent time in prison on pandering and other felonious charges. He was extremely concerned about me revealing that he's the Heidi Fleiss of the porn world.

He was very guarded about his dealings with Tim, but said he made him a lot of money because, "He had such a huge following, and men just adored him, and would do anything and pay anything to be with him." Forest said. "He had a shitload of entitlement issues. He thought the world owed him everything, He was always pissed off at one thing or another."

Chi Chi LaRue said almost the same exact thing about Tim when we talked about Tim's arrest, later on down the line. It's quite sad, the way his burned bridges can light the path to eternity.

***

So back in 2006 when Tim would go out to L.A. from Denver he would stay for three weeks, and make six thousand dollars or more, with just those few days spent doing overnights out of state. Why would he be at all interested in working any type of 9-5 job? Or be in the National Guard?

I asked him that, he said " I have a daughter, I was really trying to go straight for her sake, not really mine."

True? Who knows, that's what he said, but no way of really knowing. Tim took being an escort with a proverbial grain of salt, there were risks involved, in that someone could be 'psychotic' or go crazy. He said it was not his life ambition, but when he did it, it was a means to an end, or so he said.

He met Christina in August of 2006 and, as I've said, he started calling her his girlfriend within about two weeks, prior to his late summer trip to David Forest's house in L.A. to do his escorting. He was in love with Christina, or so he claimed and, according to him, had never been in love with a woman before her, not even Jasmine's mother.

Christina got pregnant about a month after they started dating, and he was very happy about being a father again, because he really loved children. Christina had no idea that Tim was an escort, or that he was former porno star, or that he regularly was having sex with men. When I asked him why not, he said, "Well, she would have dumped me; any girl or woman would have. None of that meant anything anyway, it was just about money and supporting myself. It didn't take away any of the feelings I had for her so why did it matter?"

The two of them found out in September that Christina was pregnant. She bought three different pregnancy tests before going to a clinic for confirmation. All three home tests came up positive. Christina was extremely nervous about being pregnant. Tim was worried too, but Christina was nervous and unsure about having a baby with Tim, whom she had only known a month at this point. They started to argue about having the baby, or terminating the pregnancy. It started to be regular arguments like every time they saw each other.

Tim did not want Christina to have an abortion as he loved children, and was happy to be having another one. Christina was a bartender, and liked to drink a lot when she wasn't tending bar. She didn't want to give up her partying ways to be a mother, especially with some guy that she hardly knew. She was going through a lot of personal issues at the same times she found she was pregnant. Her mother was battling breast cancer for a second time, so Christina was under extreme stress. She just felt at the time a baby would not have helped anyone's life at that point.

They were constantly fighting about her drinking too much and her wanting to have an abortion. Tim laid down the law and told Christina she couldn't even drink one drink. This all seemed like déjà vu after what he went through with Jasmine's mother. Tim was—according to him—very suicidal at this time. He was in love with Christina, She was pregnant with a child he wanted, but she didn't. He had a deep dark secret, and he was very fearful of her finding out about his past. He was always nervous when he went somewhere with her in public, fearful that someone would recognize him and the jig would be up.

He was really depressed about the fact that he didn't have a straight job, he would discuss his depression a lot during that time with his mother Sue Strong. She would try to encourage him that things would get better, but overall Tim viewed the relationship he was having with his mother as a very negative one.

She said, "I tried to be supportive, he wasn't really letting me in that much. I didn't know anything about his life and the escorting and certainly not the porn stuff. I didn't know any of that. He had a completely different life when he was in California."

Well, he did a lot of the escorting in Denver too. Before he ever did porn he was an escort. Susan was referring to his life away from her, but did she ever really ask him how he was making money? After all he had money to support his daughter. She said, "I always thought he made money modeling." Which he did for a time, until he deemed it, "Not enough money to feed a small bird."

Tim tried another round of doing collection work at PRS for J.P. He was starting to get really desperate at this time, he couldn't explain his traveling to L.A. for weeks at a time anymore to the now pregnant Christina. David Forest was also fed up with Tim, and said, "No matter how much he made for me, his shitty attitude wasn't worth any of the money."

So in other words, those lucrative escorting gigs through "Meet The Stars" weren't really being made available to him anymore, so it was back to J.P. and calling on debtors to pay their bills.

***

He was back to sitting in a little tiny cubicle looking for debtors to call. He lasted about two weeks this second time, but people that were trying to train him said he always seemed to have his mind on something else. They could tell he just didn't want to be there, and they were right—he didn't. He said he didn't like any of it, the searching for "all those deadbeats. Pressuring them to pay their bills, it is just a lot of pressure, I really hated it," Tim said. He would quit. "A lot of people were real nasty on the phone, and I hated just sitting there in a chair all day."

J.P. wasn't mad that Tim quit working at PRS, he accepted the fact that Tim was just not cut out to do 9-5 work and he figured he could work for him now in the way he always wanted him to. So it was not an issue for old J.P. The wheels were always turning in his head.

***

He and Tim started hanging out more after Tim quit PRS. This part of the course of events is a bit murky. The official version that Tim gave was that J.P. was depressed about his life, and he was suicidal during this time. According to Tim and the tales he spun *after* the fact, J.P. was thinking about killing himself because no one liked him, and he was always depressed and miserable. There was a tinge of truth to that perhaps. But J.P. wanting to actually take his life is almost laughable. He was never a very happy person, he had demons that he was constantly battling and people that knew him, and were willing to speak honestly about him, were the first ones to talk about his demons.

He had a very narcissistic side to him, and it was narcissism that would stop him from taking his own life. He was a very lonely person, I think at some point it's possible that J.P. did admit to himself that the only reason anyone wanted anything to do with him was because they were looking to use him. That may be harsh, but I believe it to be so, he was such a mean hateful person, I think he was to an extreme level of hate. Pure and pure unadulterated hatred filled his veins. That was from my own vantage point, what I personally saw of him.

***

Tim said on the stand that J.P. had told him he had cystic fibrosis. That turned out to be untrue, whether J.P actually told that Tim, I find very doubtful, it's possible but I don't believe based all of the information that came forward after the fact. Tim also tried to explain that J.P.

wanted to take his life because he had failed relationships shortly before he died. There were two that he talked about. One was a man much younger then J.P. by the name of Phil Hartman. It went very sour, and this is true. He was giving money to a man named Phil Hartman, and Hartman in return had sex with J.P.

Then there was another much younger man named Ron McKinney that J.P. had a commitment ceremony with. That relationship ended badly as well, with Ron taking one of J.P.'s cars and other valuable items. Tim said J.P was very happy that he actually married Ron. But Ron turned out to be an opportunist like every man J.P. was ever involved with.

J.P: was under the impression that he could buy the affections of any man he encountered. If they were of the grifter mind set like Tim and Phil Hartman, that worked for a while but always ended badly. It was a sad horrible pattern in which J.P. was immersed. Sadder was the fact that J.P. had that pattern his entire life.

With Tim, in no time, that pattern would have continued, and all of J.P. dalliances always ended badly. It was just a matter of how bad; that's what it always came down to, the degree of anger on the other side.

***

Tuesday November 7th, 2006 was the day Tim didn't report for work at PRS. The second time he quit his job there. Four days later, J.P Kelso would be dead.

The next day—on Wednesday—J.P and Tim went to the Cherry Creek Mall, and paid a visit to Blockbuster to rent some videos to watch. They watched "Little Men" at J.P.'s Congress Park home. Tim left the Kelso home at around 11 p.m. Tim claimed after that Wednesday is when J.P had asked him to help him commit suicide so his family could collect on a life insurance policy he had. That has to be an out and out lie, he hardly spoke to any of his family members which was a mother and a sister. He would never kill himself so some family member that he basically had no relationship with, could collect money on a life insurance policy. But this is the fantasy that Tim's mind came up with up for what happened in Congress Park.

***

The truth, as he admitted to me, was that he and Christina were talking about getting married. He really loved her and felt that if he asked her to marry him, there was a chance abortion would never enter her mind ever again. There was a problem with that scenario, he didn't have a job, and Christina didn't know he was a porno star, a paid escort that catered to wealthy men. She didn't know anything about his life. She thought she had this really good-looking, fine specimen of a man at her side. Yeah, he had some anger issues, and he would fly off the handle very easily, but he was under a lot stress and pressure.

***

He was starting to sway Christina over to his side of the fence when it came to getting married and keeping the baby. He put off his second stint in the National Guard, telling his recruiter he had a pregnant girlfriend and he couldn't leave her. Were all things right in Tim Boham's mind at this point in time? No not even close, he was worried and stressed out every second of every day that he was awake.

He wondered how he would support a family; he felt the walls were closing in on him.

By now, Christina was staying with him in a room in an apartment he was renting. He was trying to distance himself from J.P. Even though he knew if went over to his house and performed sexual services for him, it would bring in much needed cash, the thought of doing so was starting to make him sick. Christina didn't know any of that.

J.P knew she didn't know, he was going crazy with jealousy, he wanted Tim at his beck and call. Paying for it was nothing new for J.P.

Now paying was not an option, it wasn't enough to persuade Tim Boham to show up, no matter how much money he was offering. So when all else failed, J.P. tried out a new tactic. He flat told Tim, "Either you have sex with me, or I'll tell her, it's that simple."

Tim didn't have to ask J.P. what 'tell her' meant. He knew exactly what he meant, J.P. had a lot on Tim, he could take his pick on the dirty laundry he wanted to use. J.P said if Tim didn't acquiesce to his demands he would send Christina some of his porno flicks. Tim told him straight out to fuck off, he loved Christina and he wanted to marry her, and if J.P ever really cared for him he was respect that.

J.P. only ever cared about J.P., I believe, for whatever reasons, he was incapable of caring for another human being. Tim, a life-long gun enthusiast, always had at least one gun at his disposal. At certain periods of time he had more than one. At the time of J.P's 'death', Tim Boham had a Taurus .40 caliber gun. He took shooting classes at the Cherry Creek Gun Club in an attempt to get a concealed weapons permit. Even before he started the classes, Tim was an accomplished shot, having grown up around guns in Nebraska. His father would at times, when sober, take him on hunting trips with him.

***

A lot of things that Tim said regarding the death of J.P. were pure fabrications, conjured up to save him a trip to the electric chair. I will stick with what I believe to be the truth, based on what Tim told me personally, not what he said on the witness stand, or what he said to an attorney, although some of that must be included in these pages. All of the people Tim dealt with after the fact did not know J.P. In that aspect, I had a distinct advantage, I did know J.P. I think I was able to better discern what could have been the truth versus pure fiction. To play the devil's advocate, the others didn't know him, they didn't have a reference point to work from like I did.

***

On the days leading up to Saturday November 11th 2006, J.P started calling Tim's cell phone non-stop. He was threatening that if he didn't come over to his house, he would tell Christina about Tim's porno past. Many of those calls were made in the middle of the night, as Tim was lying in bed next to Christina. She wanted to know who was calling, and Tim sometimes told her it was a crank, but a few times he did tell her that it was J.P. calling. Tim told Christina that J.P. was openly gay, and that he kept coming on to him. That was believable, the older man was gay, and Tim was a very nice looking younger man, what young woman wouldn't believe that? It was steeped in the truth, at least that's the reason and logic that Tim used.

When J.P. turned on the heat, Tim became increasingly agitated. He wanted to go to the range and unleash his anger hastily upon a target. The Cherry Creek Gun Club was becoming a bit too much of a pricey experience. So he had to shift gears and find something cheaper. When he wasn't dodging phone calls from J.P. and acting the part of the dutiful boyfriend, he was spending a lot of time at the Shootist Pistol Range in Littleton on Galapago Street. The cost there was about half the price of the CC Gun Club.

***

While Tim was keeping his shooting skills sharp, J.P was drowning his sorrows at the La Boheme on Stout Street in downtown Denver. A typical gentlemen's club, with crappy overpriced drinks and food and girls running around looking for customers to ply them with cash. It was all just about sitting in a booth and getting drunk for J.P. He hardly looked up from his glass. He would make calls around the clock to Tim on the Thursday before the Saturday that would be J.P.'s last day alive.

***

Christina was starting to get suspicious of Tim's explanation as to why J.P. kept calling him. She didn't understand why Tim didn't just politely tell J.P. that he wasn't gay, and to please stop harassing him. Tim's inability to completely cut J.P. loose and his refusal to face the fact that Christina really didn't want to have a baby was casing the two to have even more heated arguments.

The Friday night before his death, J.P. kept calling Tim and kept asking him to come over to his house. When Tim said he couldn't, J.P. kept the pressure on. Tim finally went over to J.P.'s house around 10 p.m. on Friday only to find out that J.P. was not home. So he went back to his place, and told Christina, "Maybe he's "got it out of his system now."

In the back of his mind, he knew that J.P. would never leave him alone, and felt the walls were closing in on him. On the morning of Saturday, November 11, 2006, Tim kept getting the same threatening phone calls, and he just couldn't take it any longer. He got in his truck and drove over to Kelso's home. He walked into the house with his gun in his back pocket. He parked in the driveway, and walked through the unlocked front door. He found J.P. sitting in a recliner in his living room. He had a phone in his hand. Tim told him, "There is no reason to keep calling me, I'm here now,"

J.P. thought his blackmailing was finally paying off, there was the latest object of his affections. J.P. had been drinking. There was a mixed drink sitting on an end table by the chair he was sitting in. The TV was on, and as J.P. saw Tim, he asked him to go to his bedroom and "cuddle". Tim said "sure", the two men walked up the stairs, into J.P's master bedroom. J.P. undressed and got into his bed.

Tim stood at the foot of J.P's bed, and took his gun out of his back pocket and pointed it at J.P. He ordered J.P out of the bed. J.P. got out of the bed and sat on side of his bed.

Tim said, "I don't think you're ever going to stop blackmailing me." He told J.P. to open his safe that was in the closet.

J.P. said four words, "No way, fuck you!" and told Tim to put the gun down,

Tim said, "Open the safe, you fat bastard."

J.P. wouldn't do it.

Tim said, "Get on your knees on the floor."

J.P. did. Why he did, I don't know, but he did. Tim took the butt of the gun and hit J.P. in the head with it.

J.P. grabbed his head, and got a good amount of his own blood on his hand. He lunged at Tim, trying to get the much younger and stronger man's gun. No way that would have ever happened. At that point, J.P. tried to push an alarm panel that was in his bedroom to summon help. While he did that, Tim grabbed a pillow from the bed. He placed the pillow in the back of J.P.'s head, and lined his gun up in front of the pillow, and pulled the trigger.

That one single gunshot to the back of J.P.'s head killed him on impact. The calls, the threats, the anger instantly stopped too. Tim did not have the combination to the safe, all he had was a very large, dead, naked body in front of him.

Was he panicked? No, but he knew he needed to clean up and not leave any traces. He also needed what was in that safe so he loaded the safe into his truck. He came back inside the house and tried to move J.P.'s body and he couldn't

He tied a belt around J.P.'s ankles and dragged him into the bathroom. Tim ran the water into the tub, and once it was halfway through, he continued to drag J.P's dead body into the bathroom by pulling his legs with the help of the belt that was tied around the legs at the ankles. He lifted J.P.'s body into the tub and placed the pillow under J.P.'s chin.

Tim had cut his hands on the belt as he was dragging J.P. into the bathroom. He was hoping that the water would wipe a lot of evidence off of the body. This was a very bloody crime scene, there was blood all over that bedroom and traces of it all over the house.

As hard as Tim tried to clean the house up, there were blood and fingerprints all over the house.

Tim took some jewelry off of J.P's body rings and a necklace. He cut the belt that was used to pull J.P. with, because it had his blood on it. He cut off the pieces he thought had blood on it, then took the whole belt with him. He had already carried the safe out of the bedroom. He had thought the combination was 33-79-49, he tried it several times—that was not the combination. He then carried the safe out of the house to his vehicle.

He would return to the home on Sunday, to the home that had the body of J.P. Kelso in the bathroom bathtub decomposing. He took some more jewelry and a computer and CD's and anything else he thought he could sell for money. He tried to clean the house again.

J.P. had three small Shih Tzu dogs that Tim put in the backyard because they barked non-stop at him when he was in the house, moving around as their master's body was decomposing in the tub. It was very cold that November as the dogs stayed in the backyard for two days.

Before he went back to the house on Sunday, Tim had plans with Christina on Saturday night. These were plans that were made earlier in the week between Christina and Tim.

After he killed J.P. and cleaned up, it was close to 4 p.m. He couldn't get the safe opened with the combination he had. So he bought a saw in the Home Depot store and sawed it open. He testified there were only car titles in the safe.

I say no way; there was money in there. Why do I say that? In addition to being an alcoholic, J.P was a coke fiend. Cocaine dealers don't take checks, they want cash, and J.P. had to have cash in that safe. He had a non-stop supply of coke flowing through his veins. Any tales of car tiles and no cash are simply works of fiction that Tim devised later..

Tim took a shower, cleaned up and drove over to pick Christina up for dinner at the California Pizza Kitchen on 1st Avenue in Cherry Creek. The hands he used to eat his meal with that night were the same hands that killed J.P Kelso and dragged his dead body into his bathroom only a few hours before. The two ate dinner, and hurried along. It turned out that Tim had tickets to the Comedy Works Comedy Club on 15th Street in downtown Denver. There was no way Tim was going to miss that show; murder or no murder, 'The show just had to go on'.

***

Tim sat there with his pregnant girlfriend, drinking, eating, laughing, and just getting on with life, knowing that J.P. was rotting away in his bathroom; no one else knew that second fact. He said, "I knew it would be my last few minutes of a normal life. So I just tried to live in the moment. Not worry about tomorrow, because tomorrow was coming soon enough."

The world according to Tim Boham I suppose. A little fact; a lot fiction.

***

All day Sunday Tim spent cleaning up at J.P's house, he took off some rings from his victim's fingers, and anything else that wasn't nailed down. He threw a lot of things from J.P's house into holes in the mountains and some in Cherry Creek—some bloody towels, clothes—things he thought he couldn't sell. He also got rid of the gun.

According to Tim, on Monday the 13th. He went to his mother's home in Aurora, Colorado. There he found his mother Susan Strong and his older sister Kathrynne Boham. He told the two women that he had killed his boss; it started out as robbery and it went very bad. His mother Susan tried to reason with her son. She told him, "If you did this, please call the police and turn yourself in.

***

The next day, he kissed his girlfriend goodbye for the day, not telling her anything about his part in J.P.'s murder. He bought himself a one-way ticket to Los Angeles, with a stop in Phoenix, and headed off to the largest airport in the United States—Denver International Airport in Denver—and high-tailed it out of the 'Mile High City'. It may have been a mile high but for Tim Boham there were a million reasons not to stick around. Maybe not quite a million but enough reasons to not miss his flight.

Chapter Ten

Jail, Court, Conviction

Tim went to his mother's house on Monday after the weekend murder, and told both his mother and sister Katheryn that he killed his 'boss' J.P. Kelso. They weren't sure if he was telling the truth or not. They really didn't know what to think. Tim told the two that it was a robbery gone bad. He said he was so upset, and now he was going to go to jail for the rest of his life. His mother, Susan Strong, told her son to go to the police if that was in fact true. She was hoping against hope that what her son was saying was a lie. After all, Tim had lied to her on many occasions in the past, hopefully this was a lie too.

Unfortunately for Susan Strong this wasn't a lie, her son had in fact killed Kelso, a robbery gone bad; or so it seemed.

The story that Tim told publically was that Kelso killed himself because he wanted his own family to get the insurance money. These two versions were both told by Tim. The robbery story before during and after his arrest the suicide by Kelso on the stand.

Were either of those stories true? I don't believe so, based on what I personally know, I think the robbery was an afterthought. The Kelso committing suicide for the purpose of his family that he never talked to getting insurance money story, pure fiction.

Tim left his mother's home in Aurora, and tried to get rid of as much evidence as he could. He was nervous, he was scared and he wanted to put as much distance between himself and the house of horrors in Congress Park. I have written earlier that I was told that J.P was dead by my friend Tim Walkup. I repeat certain passages to assure the reader has a clear understanding of events as they occur.

Walkup called me Sunday night, and said "Guess who's dead?" I asked "Who?" He said "J.P. Kelso." There had been nothing on the news the night before. I asked Walkup when was Kelso killed. He said that he wasn't sure, "But he is dead." He also said he thought it may have been a robbery, although the information he had was murky at best.

I asked him how he knew that J.P. was dead. Tim Walkup said that Kelso's secretary had called him, and told him. I thought it was strange as there was nothing on TV about Kelso's death, I thought it would have been on the news.

Walkup said, "Well I don't think many people know he's dead yet."

Tim Walkup, who had been on occasion in J.P's home, said he "couldn't believe the slimy parasite was dead."

I said, "I wonder if he finally pissed off the wrong person." I added, "That's exactly what happened," even though I said that half in jest. The next night, the news in Denver did report on the death of J.P. Kelso at his Congress Park home. They reported it as a perhaps a robbery gone bad, but said it was too early to say what happened. However it was made very clear that J.P. was killed in his home. Tim Walkup and I talked about Kelso's death at length on that Monday. Although we had no knowledge, that was the same day that Tim Boham was at his mother's home confessing he in fact killed Kelso.

I went to Walkup's downtown Denver office on that Monday. An office J.P had visited when Walkup and he were making deals concerning bought debt. The Denver Post was sitting on a desk, I picked it up to see if Kelso's death was mentioned. It was and I read the article in its entirety. I looked at Walkup and said, "What do you think happened? Do you think it was a robbery?"

He said, "If it were anyone else, sure, but with J.P. anything is possible."

That's exactly what I was thinking, a robbery just didn't make sense. How often did robberics occur in Denver where someone was killed during the robbery? Seldom, it happened but I wasn't buying a robbery, I felt there had to be more.

Kelso's housekeeper, Brent Cox had showed up to clean Kelso's house on Monday morning. Like he did every Monday morning after having the weekend off. He noticed J.P's car in the driveway, which was rare, as J.P should have been at his down Denver office at that hour. He walked through the house calling 'Hi and Hello'. Cox received no response. He also noticed that Kelso's three smallish Shih Tzu dog's were outside, which was also a bit off. They were normally in the house when he got there. Cox still proceeded to bring his cleaning supplies into the home, and put them on the kitchen counter. Another thing he recalled that was odd, was that there were no dirty dishes in the sink, or empty bottles of booze anywhere. That was very odd for Monday morning.

Cox was used to seeing a sink full of dirty dishes, empty liquor bottles strewn about. When he walked up to the second floor of the house, he walked into Kelso's master bedroom suite. He saw that the bedding was half pulled off the bed, he noticed blood all over the carpet and on the walls. The bathroom door was a little ajar, but not completely open. He went into the bathroom, and saw a naked J.P. Kelso with his head on a pillow, in a bathtub full of water.

He ran down the steps of the home, and out the front door, and sat on the curb in front of the house. He contemplated going back in the house and checking on J.P. But he didn't, he knew he was dead, he dialed 911. He said "I'm a housekeeper, I found my employer dead in his bathtub. Send someone over here right away. I'm sitting in front of the house on the curb".

The police arrived after the fire department and an ambulance, some patrol officers at first. They quickly determined there was foul play and called for a CSI team and detectives to arrive on the scene. The detectives arrived and got a statement from Cox, and determined that Cox was in no way responsible for Kelso's death. It was right around this time, or shortly after the police arriving at Kelso's home that Susan Strong called 911 and reported that her son, Timothy John Boham, told her that he killed a man, his boss J.P. Kelso. Strong told this to the police. The police had some questions for her, and they let her know they would be stopping by. They had to do some research first. They did a background check on one Timothy John Boham, they pulled some pictures, and stopped off at an adult book store on Colfax Ave, before going to the Strong home.

When the arrived at the home, they asked if Susan Strong knew where Marcus Allen was right now. She said, I don't know a Marcus Allen, my son's name is John, he goes by his middle name 'John' she told the detectives. They said "Well, ok, but what about Marcus Allen?" She just looked puzzled as she said "Who is that? I don't know anyone with that name." They wanted to know if she had a DVD player, to which showed them where it was. They put in one of Tim's porn flicks, and waiting for a scene of Boham looking straight on, and said to Mrs. Strong "Is that your son?" She just sat down in a chair and looked at her son on the screen. She knew it was her son, and she was devastated to learn that he was in fact living a double life.

Not only did Susan learn that her son was doing porn, he was a big star in the gay porn world. He had a huge following, fans from all over the world watched his films, and wrote him letters, and followed his life. Even worse then Tim's porn past being exposed to his mother, was the fact that her son was now a wanted man. He was wanted for the murder of J.P. Kelso. Susan was hoping against hope that Tim who was a known liar, was lying this time too. She was really hoping that he really didn't kill J.P. She called the police because she was concerned about her son's welfare, not because she thought he really killed anyone, or so she claimed. Much later down the road, she would confess to me, that if she could hit stop and press rewind, she would have never called the police on her own son, killed someone or not. She regretted that she made that call and will have to live with that choice the rest of her life.

***

The detectives wanted to know where Tim Boham was, his mother did not know. They had a warrant for his arrest, and they wanted him. Susan said when and if she talked to him, she would tell him to turn himself in. He did call her, and she did tell him that the police were there and he should turn himself in and face the music. Tim would have no part of that when he called and would end up hanging up on his mother. Tim was on his way to Los Angeles. Knowing the police had already been to his mother's house, he decided that he would not go on to L.A. *Too risky,* he thought. Tim held a plane ticket from Denver to Los Angeles. There was a layover in Phoenix. It was in Phoenix that Tim decided to just leave the airport and not get on the connecting flight to Los Angeles.

He had no real plan when he left the airport, he asked around and decided to take a cab to Lukeville, AZ. That was about 150 miles from Phoenix. So what was there, one may ask. Well, Mexico was on the side of Lukeville, and

Mexico was looking pretty good to Tim Boham right about then. Lukeville is just a border town, where people come into US from Mexico, and Americans go into Northern Mexico. The cab fare from the Phoenix Airport to Luceville was 300 dollars. Tim got in a cab and took his small bag, and J.P.'s laptop that he stole and off he went to the boarder. It turned out to be exactly 150 miles and took about a little less than three hours to get there. The cab driver had no idea that the young clean-shaven man sitting in the back of his cab was wanted for first degree felony murder, although the driver would later say it wasn't the first time he was taking someone to the boarder, who was running away from something. He said, "Thank God for the runners, I would eat a lot less if it weren't for the runners."

So Tim got out of the cab right at the border, he gave the cab driver a 20.00 dollar tip, and off he went. With his driver's license he was able to get into Mexico. He went to a small rundown motel in Sonoyata, Sonora, Mexico, and checked himself in. He tried to get on the internet with the stolen lap top but couldn't. He mostly walked around and drank cheap Mexican beer, and kept to himself. The area that Tim was in was not a place that most Americans regularly flocked to.

He had about two thousand dollars cash on him. He could have survived for a while, and so he thought about his plight. He was able to call his mother once while he was in Mexico. She told him that the police wanted him to turn himself in. She gave him a phone number to a Denver Police Detective, Aaron Lopez. Tim wasn't sure if he would call Lopez but he took the number and put it in his wallet. He was starting to get anxious being holed up in the motel, the more he drank the more paranoid he became. He was starting to think everyone in the small little town he was in knew who he was and why he was there. He was certain someone recognized him and was going to turn him in. He heard all the horror stories about doing time in Mexican jails.

On November 16th he checked out of his motel and headed back to the border in Lukeville. He successfully crossed the border back into the United States.

1.

Now back in Arizona, he was in a bit of quandary, he used his cell phone to call Lopez and told him he was in Arizona, and will probably be turning himself in, but he wasn't positive, he told the detective. He was able to now get on the internet, he googled his name, and like Christmas his image lit the screen. There he was 'former male porn actor wanted in the murder of Denver businessman John Paul

Kelso'. He kept lingering around the border check-in gate, even though he successfully crossed back over.

The border patrol agents started to grow suspicious of this young man who appeared to be lingering about. Tim was terribly paranoid but he was not mistaken now when he noticed the immigration agents staring at him. They were indeed staring at him. Tim walked over to one of them and said "I think there is a warrant out for me, and I want to turn myself in."

The agent looked at Tim and asked what state was the warrant from, what for and what was his name. He responded " Timothy John Boham, Colorado, first degree murder." A quick search by the agent confirmed the information as correct. Tim was taken into custody at the boarder crossing at Lukeville, AZ on November 16th 2006, three days after he murdered J.P. Kelso in Denver.

He was interviewed in a small holding cell in the guard shack. He basically told the police that he killed J.P. by accident, "That it was a robbery gone bad." He was told that some Denver detectives were in route to Arizona. The Colorado police arrived in Arizona later that day. Tim was arraigned the next morning in a Phoenix, Arizona courtroom. He waived his right to appeal his extradition to Colorado. Tim along with Detective Aaron Lopez and another officer took Tim back to Denver by car. He was booked into the Denver County Jail on November 17th 2006. He was being held on first degree murder charges, without bail, he would be spending the next two and half years here on Smith Road in Denver, while he fired attorney after attorney and tried to come up with something logical to tell a jury. The truth never entered Tim's mind, lie after lie was the running plan.

When the news broke that Tim had been arrested in Arizona by the Mexican border, and was extradited back to Colorado, I started to listen very closely. I knew that since Tim was an ex-porn star, there had to be sex involved in this sad tale. I wanted to know what happened exactly, I knew I would never know, unless I went directly to the source. Which in this case was the accused who was locked up on Smith Road. I wrote him a note, I said I knew J.P. He wasn't the saint everyone is making him out to be, he was a mean nasty bastard, so if you need some help regarding what his character was like, when he was alive let me know. He called me a few days later, and said 'This is John Boham and any and help you could give me, would be great." I went to Smith Road to visit Tim Boham. I had a visit with him on November 20th 2006. He was just so polite, that's what was so noticeable about him. Hard to believe he was the big bad menacing porno star.

Smith Road Jail, Denver, Colorado

I asked him about his name, and he said he's always gone by his middle name of John. I said, "Oh, well, I'm starting to read a lot of the reports in this case and since J.P. is called John sometimes, can I call you Tim?"

He said, "You can call me whatever you like, that's the least of my problems right now." So thereafter I called him Tim and referred to him as such. I told him I was a writer, and I would be writing about the case, he just said "Ok, just get it right."

I cut right to the chase and said, "So, J.P. was an old, ugly, fat, bloated queen. Why were you with him?"

He laughed and said, "He really wasn't that bad."

I said, "Yeah, he was."

He tried to convince me that he and J.P. had this really great friendship, and they had a great time hanging out and doing things. It was hard for me to keep a straight face as he was saying this.

I told him I knew all about J.P. And his penchant for young good-looking men, I saw it. I told him that I once worked for him at PRS. He said "Oh yeah, I worked at that pit too". I told Tim that it definitely wasn't the happiest place on earth.

I spoke to the warden at the jail and told her that I was helping Tim do some legal research for his case, so I needed privacy. She allowed me to have legal visits with him. Which was nice, because the visits were not monitored by correctional officers and they afforded the privacy that a 'normal visit' didn't. A visit with inmates at this jail consisted of the visitor looking into a TV screen, and talking into a phone, and the inmate doing the same on the other end of the screen.

I was able to avoid all of that. Tim talked about the porn business he couldn't get away from fast enough. He said the money was intoxicating. As he put it "What other job can you get paid to do, what you're going to do anyway?" Not many I told him.

He said "I liked having sex, and was having it, getting paid to do it, was really no big deal after a while."

"Apparently," I told him. If he was embarrassed that he was a porn star or that he made porn, he didn't show it during my visits with him. He talked about it, like it was nothing. The hardest part of the job according to Tim was, "all the people I had to work with that were sick."

By sick he meant had AIDS or HIV or other STD's. He said as soon as he got to the jail in Denver, he told one of the guards, "You know who I am, test me, I would be interested to know, and I'll be shocked if I'm not dying of something I caught on a movie set." He said he was tested and to his knowledge everything came back negative.

I said, "Boy the irony of that – you made it out without any permanent party favors, a feat few do, but you couldn't stand clear of that slimy old queen, and avoid getting pissed off enough at him to kill him." I'm sure that as I said that, a smile must have crossed my face, because he said, "That's really not funny." I said, "It's a little funny, more ironic then funny, but very funny actually."

I told him that a lot of people over the years wanted to kill J.P. He had a lot of people that he crossed paths with, that didn't like him very much.

He said, "Well, that's surprising, he was actually a very nice guy."

I guess I wasn't in the cutting slack kind of mood. I said to him, "Gee, what happens to people you think are horrible mean shameless bastards?"

He found that very funny and started laughing. I mentioned Chi Chi LaRue to Tim. I said, "Chi Chi goes around the media calling himself the 'Condom Nazi'; he says that's a big deal to him, that condoms always be used."

Tim said "That is just not true. I rarely if ever saw condoms, and that was one of the biggest reasons I left. It got to the point where most people on a set were HIV positive, or some had full blown AIDS. They were sitting around sick and coughing and I was just expected to be there doing scenes with these people. Make up was used to cover up legions and 'On with the show'. It was sick and I was sick of doing it. I wanted better for myself so my little girl would be proud of me, not ashamed of her father."

We talked about the public defenders that were assigned to him. Stephen Flavin was the senior attorney in the public defenders' office at that time. Tim said he was a "stupid prick, that couldn't be bothered about anything. With him 'helping' me, I'm going to straight to the chair." Tim kept saying he was going to try to prove he was insane at the time of the shooting. He said he and the lawyers were after a "NGR' plea. meaning a not guilty by reason of insanity.

I told him those types of pleas are seldom successful. Most of the people that have been successful using that plea are those people with long-term documented mental illness and namely schizophrenic deviations.

Tim had many things on his mind during those visits in the late fall of 2006. He was very concerned about his girlfriend, Christina Hernandez who, last time he knew, was pregnant with his second child.

I asked him what the status of their relationship was on that day.

He said, "Well, she of course didn't know about me, not the real me anyway. To find out the way she did in a single second was very hard, and she really doesn't talk to me or my family."

"What happened with the baby?" I asked him. He said he didn't know and had a favor to ask of me. He wanted me to find if Christina was still pregnant. I asked him how was I going to do that, did he have a phone number for her, where was she now etc. He really didn't know much, he said she was from San Diego, and that's where her family was. He said she came to Denver to go to school but dropped out shortly after starting, and just stayed in Denver.

I asked him how pregnant she would be, he said about 4 months, maybe 5 now. I knew she was a bartender at the Purple Martini in Downtown Denver when he met her. I told Tim I would try my best, to find her and find out what happened to the baby. I told him I would try to find out from her. The next night I grabbed a friend of mine, and we headed to the Purple

Martini to snoop around. I was able to talk to a server there that knew Christina well. She informed me that right after Tim was arrested and after she visited Tim in jail, (her first and last time) she had an abortion. She said she had no qualms about having an abortion. "What life would a child of a killing gay porno star have?" Christina reportedly said. I knew that news would be upsetting,

Tim called me the next day. I informed him that after Christina had a visit with him, she had an abortion. I also found out that shortly after she had the abortion she moved back in with her parents in San Diego.

Tim was very upset, he said, "She "had no right to do that."

I said, "Well, Tim, you were a porno star, you were doing your escorting while you were dating her. You were having sex with men for money while you were dating her. She didn't know any of that, then she finds out you killed someone. Almost any young woman would have done the same exact thing, not all but a lot. I told him he should focus on his upcoming trial, and trying to get out of a life sentence. He, on a daily basis, was firing attorneys, and trying to hire new ones, and or was acting as his own attorney. His case was a mess, there was no clear path, no real direction.

I asked him what exactly happened on one of my visits. He looked at me and asked "What do you think happened?"

I just said I didn't know, I said, "Maybe he did something that made you mad, or you did something that made him mad, and things got out of hand and one thing led to another and he wound up dead, and you wound up running for your life."

He said, "Well, I desperately needed money; she was pregnant, I wasn't really working anywhere. I could have figured out things, but he would wait until it was late at night and we were both sleeping and then call non-stop."

I was a little confused so I asked him about all that.

He said "Well, he would call me up in the middle of the night and threaten me. He would say come over and fuck me, or I'm going to tell your girlfriend you're a fag, and a porno star, etc. etc. etc. He actually threatened to send her my movies, I was besides myself with his calls. I was in love with Christina. In my mind, the past was the past, it didn't matter. We were going to have a baby and get married, she didn't have to know about the past, that part of my life was over."

I asked him if perhaps he ever thought about coming clean and just telling her the truth, especially when J.P. started to make his threats. He said he did think about it, but just knew she wouldn't except it, and he was very afraid of losing her. I said why not go to the police, it was classic black mail what he was doing to Tim, why not just turn him in.

Tim said, "Well, I thought about that too, but I just didn't think they would listen to me or care or side with me. I was the porno star, he was the respected businessman."

Was I surprised that J.P. was threatening Tim in the way it was described by someone who could have been facing the electric chair? No I wasn't surprised at all and it sounded very plausible to me, as far as what lengths J.P. would have gone through to get what he wanted.

Tim Boham was taking a beating in the press. He was a hustler, a a gay porn star, a really horrible despicable human being, that J.P had the misfortune of coming into contact with. The case got a lot of press in Denver, and in certain quarters around the country. The gay community was on the case quite a bit as it was unfolding. Mostly because Tim did gay porn, and had a huge fan base within the gay community. The

'Advocate' and 'Frontier' ran stories on updates of the case. That brought up another interesting conundrum, what was Tim Boham's sexual inclinations?

I asked straight out, "Are you bi? Are you gay? Are you in denial?" Before I asked him that, I watched some of his movies, I couldn't watch them in their entirety but I did watch them to get a feel for what it was Tim did exactly. We are talking about triple X films here, very hardcore pornography.

I would go to the jail on Smith Road, and Tim would say, "So how was your night?"

One day I said, "Huum, quite interesting, I watched 'Never Been Touched' last night."

He would turn beet red and say, "Oh you shouldn't watch that. That's not something I'm proud of." I'm sure he wasn't proud of it, and it embarrassed him and he was in a very dark place and sat in his cell and was haunted by the bad choices that he made.

I find it all terribly sad, he was a nice kid, very polite, and very smart, and I think at the core a pretty good person. The problem was the core was buried so deep, it was anyone's guess as to if that core could ever be located again. He was such a damaged soul by the time I started to visit him in jail. I don't think he became damaged just because of what happened to J.P. I think there was a lot of collateral damage that had added up prior to the murder.

At the same time I was visiting Tim in jail I was getting to know his family too. I had long conversations with his mother Susan Strong and his sister Katheryn Boham. I thought maybe getting his story out there, and talking about the good qualities he had would be a good idea. So I contacted a TV show that was on PBS, called 'Colorado Outspoken'. It's a show that centered around issues affecting the LGBT community in Colorado. They let me know they wanted to do a show about Tim's case. I told Tim about it, and he was glad that a different side of the tale would finally be told. I also told him that, "I think your mom should go on the show with me."

Susan Strong didn't want to do the show, she was very apprehensive, and it seemed like no amount of convincing would change her mind. The show was shot at a studio in Golden, not far from 'Coors'. I signed on, and it was starting to look like just me and the moderator, Daryl Johnson. So I headed over to the studio in early April of 2007, and while in route, Susan called me and said Tim convinced her to be on the show. I gave her directions to the studio, and with her daughter and husband Walter Strong she arrived at the Golden studio. We were wired for sound, and sat at table with Daryl Johnson and answered questions about Tim mostly. I talked a bit about J.P. I was very careful in my remarks about him. I just said a lot of what was being said in the media about him is just not true.

Intended for Mature Audiences/Donna Thomas

Susan Strong on Colorado television

Susan talked about Tim's humble beginnings in the tiny town of Stuart Nebraska.

A neighbor of Tim's in Denver, Laura Holland was telling the media that Tim told her he hated gays, and scrubbed his apartment because he was afraid gay people may have lived there. I asked Tim about that, he said " I never said that, why would I even say such a thing? Let's say I did do that I wouldn't ever announce that's what I did. She had a crush on me, and even asked me out on a date, I told her I had a girlfriend. I think that's why she said it. She couldn't get over the fact that I turned her down."

Anything was possible, Susan used the show as an opportunity to cast aspersions on Laura Holland's story. Susan went on to tell tales of Tim's love of gays, and told a story of a big beef hot dog, which Tim ate at a fair. After the fact it seemed like her story had some sort of double meaning, and it probably would have went off better if she left that little tidbit out. But she wasn't media savvy and was very nervous and did and said what she thought would be most favorable for her son.

No one can fault a parent for trying to save a child from the worst possible fate. I told Tim the show went well, and it was a good thing that Susan was on the show. I wanted to know if he went over to J.P's house to kill him or if after he got into the safe, did they struggle for the gun? What happened? I also knew that Tim was spinning one lie after another in this case. I didn't believe for a second that they fought over a gun, I didn't believe his sole reason for going to J.P.'s house was to just get a safe, or have J.P. open a safe. I was starting to think that J.P. did in fact call Tim in the middle of the night when he was lying in bed with Christina, and asked him to come over, and if he didn't he made all kinds of threats. The threatening texts were admitted into evidence at Tim's trial.

Tim one day just said, "I was going over there to ask him to stop making threats, I asked him if he only cared about his own happiness and not mine or anyone's."

I said, "Well "I could have saved you some time on that, he only cared about himself he was a real shameless bastard."

"Yes I know," said Tim. " I wanted to make it very clear that he couldn't blackmail me, or make threats, I threatened him with bodily harm, 'Either shut your fucking mouth or I'll kill you'." I wanted his money too. He told me that they did struggle for the gun and it accidentally went off. I didn't believe that, and I told him I didn't believe it.

He asked me why I didn't believe him, I said, "I know you're lying, because if you went there to take money or rob him at gunpoint, you would have known that he would have turned you in, and there was no way you were going to be turned in, I believe that you went there because he was blackmailing you. You wanted to take everything you could carry out of that house, and after you got it out, you were going to shoot him to death no matter what else happened."

He said, "None of that matters, I got to prove I was crazy so I can get off."

"I know you did it in cold blood," I told him, "and I know you're sorry – maybe not that you did it but that you got caught and you're here."

He just shook his head, and started crying. He basically confirmed that he went there to make him stop blackmailing him permanently and steal everything that was not nailed down. He told the police that he carried J.P.'s small safe out of the house, bought a saw at Home Depot and sawed the safe open, and there was no money in that safe.

I call that bull. J.P. Kelso was a coke head, who drank a lot and did a lot of coke. Coke dealers don't take checks and they don't take credit cards, they do take money and lots of it, and that is how I know there was a lot of money in that safe. The cab ride from Phoenix to Lukeville was three hundred dollars alone. After all, Tim had shot and killed J.P. execution style, one bullet to the back of the head. He went back to the house on Sunday cleaning away finger prints, and stealing any and everything that wasn't nailed down. He also took jewelry off of J.P.'s dead body, as he layed naked and dead in his bathtub. Tim dragged J.P.'s body to the bathtub after he shot him in his bedroom, J.P. was kneeling down at the foot of his bed. Tim had hit J.P. on the head with the butt of his gun, before he started kneeling on the floor, he did that to try to get him to give him the combination to the safe. When he refused and tried to hit an alarm on the bedroom wall, Tim took a pillow from the bed, put it in front of the barrel of his gun and pulled the trigger into the back side of J.P.'s head, it killed him instantly, he picked up the shell casing from the discharged bullet, and put it in his pocket."

He took a belt and tied it around J.P.'s ankles and dragged J.P.'s dead body into the bathroom and then put him into his bathtub, and he filled the tub with water, he placed the pillow under J.P.'s chin. It took six Denver police officers to get J.P.'s body out of the tub.

I recited these events again to Tim and he said, "Yeah that's basically what happened." Tim would spend the next almost two years trying to come up with a reasonable story that a jury would believe and then set him free.

After a jury was seated, Tim's first degree murder trial would begin on June 1, 2009 in Denver. He had two private attorneys, both women, Amber St. Clair and Kristan Wheeler representing him. Both of them received stipends from the state of Colorado to represent Tim. The state had two prosecutors, Bonnie Benedettti and Diane Balkin, that latter of which, appeared on the TV show 'Deadly Sins' on the ID Discovery Channel, with me and Chi Chi LaRue, during a show about the case.

Tim would be taking the stand in his own defense. He would contend that what happened was he agreed to help J.P. commit suicide so that his family (J.P's family) could collect insurance money. His only real relatives were a sister and mother who he barely spoke to. Tim's mother, sister and Christina all took the stand and testified against him. Tim spoke of his work as an escort, his problems with his family, Christina. Little of what he said on the stand was true. Everything he said about the murder was a lie.

Chapter 10

Varying Accounts, Varying Versions!

Depending on who was telling the story, the accounts as it related to this story vary quite a bit in some instances. Even accounts of J.P. Kelso's character are different from person to person. He definitely had a few different sides to him. I wouldn't say a lot but a few. I think he was a lot easier to figure out then the varying accounts indicate. My initial general impression I got from him, was that he didn't like women at all, he didn't respect them. He was a lot nicer to the men that crossed his path than he was to the women. He had no use for women, and he said that basically. I think it may have something to do with the fact that he didn't get along with his mother, and the two barely spoke. Suzanne Berbert, a tiny frail-looking woman, sat in the court room nearly every day during the trial of Tim J. Boham, the man accused of the first degree murder of her son J.P. Kelso. It was sad to watch her, she undeniably was in a lot of pain, that was very obvious.

What was she looking for in that courtroom? The answers about her son that she was unable or unwilling to get during his life? J.P. was openly gay, there were no denials or fake relationships with women, no children. I did have respect for him in that regard. Look at all the men that play it straight, and bring innocent children and sometimes women into the mix, just to hide their true selves. J.P. didn't do that, and because there are so many that do, I always respect those that live their true selves.

However in J.P's case it caused a lot of alienation from his family members, his mother being one of them. His sister Kimberly MacLaren was also said to be very estranged from J.P. I reached out to people in the credit and collection industry in Denver and the surrounding areas, to see if someone wanted to share some memories they had of J.P. with me. One - a Mr. Edward Oakhome who owns a collection agency in South Denver, said he had known J.P for many years. Edward had fondly recalled that J.P. gave him his start in the collection industry.

He said J.P. hired him right out of college. He said he learned all the ropes from J.P. He was a hard worker that instilled a good work ethic in everyone around him." Edward also said, "I knew him at a very high level of business dealings and personally. J.P. was a good guy in general, with a few demons that he could never get rid of."

Well. "A few demons" is like saying Adolph Hitler killed a few people. He had the type of demons you either get rid of or they get rid of you permanently. That is exactly what happened here. Actually there are a lot of people that live the same way that J.P. did: troubled – many of them gay, lonely, rich; buying the love of someone they probably wouldn't be with if it not for the fact that person's love is bought. It's all very sad, the people like J.P. that live this type of destructive lifestyle. It's sad but more common then anyone would probably admit to.

My hat was always off to J.P. in that he didn't hide his sexuality, he was very open about it. He didn't go and get married, and bring innocent children into a charade more commonly referred to as "a marriage of convenience". There are many of those all around from Hollywood on down the line. As liberal and progressive as people in 2014 think they are, there are still people by the droves getting married to someone of the opposite sex, simply to appease their family, or fit in to societal expectations. They can be seen every day, someone walking with someone that is clearly gay, but they are sitting there married to some poor (and what I think) unsuspecting woman, that has no idea, that the person laying next to them is a maniacal disturbed pervert. Then you have to wonder about people like Kelly Preston, she has to know right? Or does she chalk it off to 'everyone is lying, or jealous or whatever."

You just wonder and if it's not that, what the hell is it then? Well, to be honest, there are more of those closet cases in Hollywood, then normal 'traditional types of marriages'. Sometimes people try very hard to suppress some of that, and just marry hoping they will change.

Or they totally embrace who they are to themselves, but are not ready to reveal anything other than a Ozzie and Harriet type of life, to the rest the world. In my opinion, that was the only saving grace that Mr. J.P. Kelso had, he was honest with who he was, and lived an authentic life, as far what his true sexuality was.

Much more so as a matter of fact than Tim Boham did. I believe that was at the core of Tim's self loathing, and there was a lot of that. Did he think that being gay was wrong because of the strong bible yielding Christian upbringing he had? More than likely yes, that was part of his anger. That anger manifested itself into an unstable angry young man, prone to fits of rage. There is no other way of honestly portraying a true picture of Tim Boham. I think his quest for women was going on for a few reasons. He knew he sexually preferred men but he didn't like that fact about himself. He was trying to change that about himself, so he —

like many others – thought if he could just carry on a romantic relationship with a woman, than he was straight.

Having a relationship with a woman would cancel out all the sex he was having with who knows how many men. Professional as porn star and as an escort, he estimated that he had probably had sex with more than two thousand men. I believe that number. I believed it now, and I believed it then. He actually initially gave me a much lower number than two thousand.

I said "Tim don't lie, come on, why lie, there is no point in lying now. I know you have had sex with more than that amount," I told him. He asked me how I knew. I said "I saw your films; not all of them but a lot of them, and I just know that that number is nonsense." So then he came with the two thousand amount. He didn't like the fact that he preferred men, and really if he could chose, he would have chosen straight, any day and Sunday. But he couldn't chose, he was left with the cold hard facts, and that was at least 2000.

He said, "Yeah, I'm sorry I don't mean to mislead you, but that's just another one of many things, I'm very embarrassed about all that. Not anyone I slept with off film but on film, yeah it's very embarrassing."

I asked about all the men he had sex with when he was an escort before and after his porn career. He said that didn't bother him because there was no permanent record of it like porn. "I can't deny the porn, it's there for everyone to see. I'm not proud of that, not of any of it. People will blush and make these little double-sided remarks, especially guys; Like: 'You're so cute', 'You're so this', 'You're so that'. Inside I'd dying a little every time I hear that, every single time I heard that."

In my opinion none of the remorse or second guessing he had for the porn industry changes what happened in Congress Park. However it makes Tim Boham seem just a smidgen more sympathetic, and that's all it would have taken: one person to find a little sympathy for him and say he wasn't guilty of premeditated murder. Then that one person could have hung a jury.

I'm not saying that I feel Tim should have been found not guilty. He should have been — he killed J.P. Kelso in cold blood. He told me he that he did the deed. He said he went there to "shut that fat pig's mouth up for good." I really do believe that the moment Tim Boham got his truck that Saturday in November of 2006, on his way to J.P.'s house, Kelso was a dead man. No matter what happened when he got there, no matter what J.P. did or said, Tim Boham was going to kill him, silence him for good. I think J.P. Kelso was everything that Tim Boham hated about himself. What did he hate about himself one may ask? What didn't he hate is a much better question.

He hated the fact that he was gay, some people are really lucky, they warmly embrace what they are, and have everyone around them that matters love them regardless of what they are. Those people are the luckiest. That's one thing that J.P. and Tim Boham did not have in common. J.P. was openly gay. Not person that knew Tim Boham prior to porn and Hollywood knew that Tim has sex with men, not one.

Additionally, not one person knew that he actually preferred having sex with men. Why didn't any of them know, some may ask? Because he made believe he was straight. He went after women and tried everything in his power to have relationships with them, and because he was a very good-looking man, he was able to easily do it. Most women of that age have no clue about any of that, they truly think if a man comes on to them and presents themselves as straight, well that's what they are.

Remember Jim McGreevy the ex-Governor of New Jersey? He stood in front of a pool of cameras and said, "I am a gay American," as his second wife Dina looked on. He knew he was gay his entire life, from the time he was a young boy, but yet he married two different women before he finally started living his authentic self. That was only after one of his lovers was blackmailing him for money. He may have never come clean and continued to live on the 'down low', which he did his entire life until that point. How many others are there like him? When you pool the high profile and the normal profile, I say millions easily. It's all over the place, in Hollywood, but in any Podunk little town and city any and everywhere. Go on any website and see how many married men are looking for men, thousands at any given time, it's a lot more prevalent than women are aware of. Men of course know, they are the ones doing it, but women are by and large extremely naive when it comes to that.

I told all of this to Tim, hopefully so that he would understand he was not alone in his charades. At the point I told him that his fate was already sealed. He was still enveloped by so much guilt, even after the fact, that perhaps I just wanted to convey a bit of sympathy to him. Yes he killed someone in cold blood, and I knew it, when I was sitting there telling him about everyone in Hollywood that was gay and pretended to be straight. I was forgetting for a moment that he was at one time a product of Hollywood. It was very easy at times to forget that fact. He was as far removed from what anyone would think a porno star would be. However most of them, are just people, it's a job to them, they don't think of it in any other way. They go to work and do their thing and make money and go home and pay their bills. A lot of them have relationships that are healthy others have very unhealthy toxic relationships with their partners. Some raise beautiful healthy, well adjust children. While others have children that are constantly in despair. How does any of that differ from any of the other millions of other people that are not adult film actors? It doesn't, it's that simple, very easy answer.

Although I do think that many adult film actors have a higher rate of drug and alcohol abuse issues. Many more percentage wise of people that were sexually abused as children venture into the adult film world. Tim estimated that it was probably 95% of the women, and maybe 60 % of the men had been sexually abused. Tim told me that most of his client base he had when he was an escort were married men, less then 5% were not married. If you think about it, men can get sex from another man very easily, without all the wining and dining that is often necessary when 'courting' a woman. So if both are just single men on the prowl for another man, would they be paying for it? Of course not, but if they are married and need secrecy, and someone that just wants cash, and doesn't care about your marriage problems, that's where to go.

So, as Tim and I were sitting in jail discussing his fate and his life and his mistakes, I did feel sympathy for him. In any other setting, he really could be the boy next door, as David Forest of 'Meet The Stars' who I have mentioned earlier told me. Forest who has quite the rap sheet himself lives in Southern California. He is a really sleazy character according to many in the know. I talked to him, he seemed perfectly friendly and pleasant. He basically facilitates the meetings of male porn stars and the men that would love to be in their company.

According to him, he just gets the two parties together, "what happens after that, is not my affair." I think that's what Heidi Fleiss once said. When Tim was between films or just needed money, he would call Forest up, and be on his roaster of available porn stars that are ready to meet their adoring fans. Forest told me that Tim/John/ Marcus – I don't know what name to use now – was really hot, a much requested star. He had a lot of fans and people just loved him, and wanted to be with him, money didn't matter, they would do anything to spend some time with him.

I asked Tim about David Forest, since it came up right on the witness stand. He said "Yeah another one of my shining moments documented on my resume."

I still felt that he was just a naive kid from Nebraska in over his head. I know some have said he was no naive kid, he was a real hustler a porno star, that killed some wonderful philanthropic all around nice guy J.P. Kelso. Maybe if I wouldn't have known J.P. and knew what he really was all about, I would have thought, *you're here because you should be here.*

I thought he was there because had the misfortune of meeting J.P. and J.P. was a despicable man on many levels. There is no way that J.P deserved to be shot in the back of his head as he was while struggling with Tim to stay alive. That's what happened that afternoon. The 44-year-old, very overweight and out-of-shape and a little drunk J.P. Kelso was in the final fight for his life. He was up against a foot and half taller Tim Boham, the one-time porn star who was almost twenty years younger than J.P.. in very physical shape, worked out daily and who left the womb angry. There was no chance for J.P.

There were actually times that I sat in Tim's jail cell with him as he was spinning his lies about what happened that day, that I would envision things. I would envision J.P. in my head, I would get a picture of him, and as Tim was telling me his lies, I knew that he was lying. There was no doubt at all for me; when he lied I knew he was lying. When it came to J.P. and that day, I could figure out what were lies and what weren't. I believe that at first he was trying to feel me out, to see how I would react to his lies, what I would say. He was a young man that had perfected the art of lying. For crying out loud, he was a big porn star, and no one in Denver knew that; they didn't know that at the time he was being booked into the county jail, he was on the cover of 'Playgirl Magazine' the very same day.

He was an expert at concealing the truth, or so he thought. He was good, but not good enough. When we were sitting there talking, Tim knew that I knew J.P., that I had once worked for him. He said to me, "What did you think of him?" I asked if he wanted the truth, and he said he did. "I thought he was a fucking bastard, he was a miserable screaming queen, he hated women, he had no use for them, he treated them like dogs, or they were invisible to him. His eyes danced with joy when a good-looking young guy walked past him. I'm surprised it took this long for someone to put that weasel out of his misery. That's what I thought of him, and I was far from alone in those thoughts."

I guess he wasn't expecting that type of answer, but a very broad smile crossed his face, and he started opening up a lot more about old J.P. Kelso. He knew I didn't like him at that point, so I guess his proverbial gloves came off.

After that little 'pep talk' I said, "OK he did something or said something to piss you off, you went over there to put that weasel out of his misery, right?"

He said" Yeah he was threatening to tell Christina that I was in the porn business and that I did guys, something like that, he was calling me and texting me constantly at all hours to cause fights between her and I. I was so fucking angry at him I wanted to kill him. I did. I couldn't stand it anymore, I was afraid I would lose her and never see my baby, and I didn't want to lose my family. I really did love her, I wanted to have another kid, I loved my daughter, I wanted another kid, I love kids, I always wanted to have a lot of kids. He was trying to ruin that for me, I was sick of his shit."

The initial police reports were that J.P.'s death was "A robbery gone bad." However it was not that. It was about money after the fact, but before the fact, it was about unbridled anger. Tim, by all accounts, was impulsive and had absolutely no impose control. When provoked even a little, the filters were completely off. On the witness stand during the trial, Tim did take the stand in his defense. He was asked of course all about the night that he killed J.P. What really happened and what he said happened did not even closely resemble the truth. Tim had told me before the trial that he was heavily leaning toward NGI defense. A not guilty by reason of insanity.

There was testimony during the trial that Tim was overheard talking on jail phones about "playing crazy". He never told me that on the phone, but in person he did. I think a not guilty by reason of insanity would have been a plausible defense. I don't think that was the real case, but it was closer to the truth than the rubbish that Tim told on the stand.

He went through so many attorneys prior to his June 2009 trial, that's hard to keep track of all of them. He was first represented by Stephen Flavin, a seasoned Denver public defender. The two butted heads constantly, most because Tim thought he knew the law better and was just a lot smarter than Flavin. Well, Flavin may have not been one of the nicest people on the planet, but he certainly knew his way around a courtroom, and he knew the law. Not to Tim Boham or AKA Marcus Allen; he just knew it all, and before too long Flavin would be toast. Colorado has funds available to use for getting indigent defendants private attorneys versus public defenders. He ended up with Amber St. Clair and Kristan Wheeler. They may have been in a little over their heads, the state had Bonnie Bendetti and Diane Balkin.

I was on a TV show with Balkin, discussing the case. She was very articulate and very thorough. If she is going to argue a case, she is going to do her homework thoroughly. Before the trial his attorneys contacted me, to see what impact I had on Tim and on J.P. and what I believed the dynamics of the two were. Balkin and Bendetti were skilled and well versed trial attorneys, Tim's lawyers had their work cut out for them.

I told an investigator for the defense that Kelso was blackmailing Tim, he was threatening him and harassing him on a daily basis. I was asked how I knew that, I told the investigator that Tim told me that, and it definitely sounds like something J.P. would do. I told her I believed that was the truth. I really believed, from my conversations with Tim, his defense team and his mother Susan, that the defense would use that as their position. That he was being blackmailed, he asked J.P. to stop, and he snapped, or something along those lines. When the time came for the defense to put on their case, I was shocked at what I heard Tim say on the stand. Since Tim was claiming what he did, he had to take the stand. Not that he had to legally but there was really no way out of him getting up on that stand and pleading his case.

On June 4th 2009 Tim took the stand in his own defense. Judge William Hood presided over the courtroom. The judge asked Tim if he understood that he did not have to take the stand. Tim said he did, he was also asked by the judge if he was making the decision to testify on his free will, Tim said that he was. He took the stand and was sworn in. Judge Hood asked the routine question, Are you under the influence of alcohol, drugs, or medication today? Tim said no. He asked him Do you suffer from any mental disorder or psychological problem which is affecting your ability to think clearly today? Tim replied that he wasn't, so in other words he was fit as a fiddle. He said his name was Timothy John Boham, but that to most people that know him he goes by his name of John.

Tim's attorney Amber St. Clair would be doing the direct examination by the defense. Tim got on the stand, and was asked his name. He said

Timothy John Boham. St. Clair asked him what name he went by, he replied that most people that know him well call him by his middle name, John. St. Clair asked him about Kelso, what he called him. Tim said he called him John, and she asked if there was another name he went by, Tim said, J.P.

Q: Okay. Let's cut to the chase. Do you feel you're responsible for the death of J.P. Kelso?

A: Yes

Q: What do you mean by that?

A: I mean, that if not for me giving J.P. my weapon or supplying that weapon for him, that he would be alive today.

Q: Okay

A: Possibly, I mean, at least he wouldn't have done it that day.

Q: Let's go into the specifics of that, okay? I want to go back in time, ask you about when you first met. I am going to call him J.P. That's what we have been calling him throughout the trial. Are you okay with that? Would you understand when I refer to him as J.P. Kelso?

A: Yes.

Q: How long before this date you have J.P. Kelso?

A. I first met J.P. in, like, probably 2004, the end of 2004 or beginning of 2005.

Q: What were the circumstances?

A: I had—I had a Taurus Sho that had a manual transmission, and was driving back from Nebraska where I picked up my daughter, and the transmission... the clutch had gone out. I made it back to North Denver area and I called my friend Bill to—to ask for a ride and he showed up in a Jeep Cherokee and J.P was with him.

I wasn't sure at that moment in court why he lied about how and when he met J.P. However before too long I would find out the exact reason why.

Q: Did you have much of a relationship or friendship with J.P. at that time?

A: No.

Q: Okay. Did you see J.P. ever again after that day?

A: Yes

Q: Tell us about that.

A. Someone named Dan called me, asked me to come down to 'Shotgun Willies', (a very well know Denver strip joint), and they weren't there. And I called Dan, and he said they were over at J.P.'s house.

Q: Where was J.P.'s house?

A: Over on 7th--7th and Colorado, close to there.

Q: Same house that he had on the date of November 13, 2006?

A: Yes.

Q: Okay. So did you go over to J.P.'s house?

A: Yes, I did.

Q: Tell us about that:

A: I went over there. Dan and—I knew him as John - If I go ahead and say John, is that all right? John was there and Dan and another younger guy there, and they said that they were going to have some strippers come over there for the after party.

Q: So did you guys hang out that night?

A: Yeah. We hung out a little bit.

Q: Did you get to know each other?

A: Not really, you know, just, you know, had a couple of conversations, you know I mean, we—I didn't stay there very long so---

Q: How did—what is the next time you saw him? Instead of going through a whole year of stuff, let me just ask you, did you develop a friendship with him at some time?

A: Yes I did.

Q: Let's be honest, for what?

A: Dan wanted me to go over there for an escort.

Q: Okay. Keep going.

A: And I ended up meeting J.P., and I ended up giving J.P. my number, and we started hanging out after that.

I believe based on what I was told by Tim, all of that—as to how he met J.P. was pure lies. He met him at a coffee shop on Colfax Ave. Tim was unemployed looking through want ads of the Denver Post. J.P. saw him and recognized Tim from his porn flicks and came over to him and started a conversation with him, and gave him his card. I don't know who came up with what, or for what reason, but Tim's porn career was not mentioned during his trial, not one word about it. Neither the defense nor the prosecution brought it up. I was sitting in the courtroom stunned at the retelling of how Tim met J.P. I knew what I was hearing was a lie.

Next question by St. Clair was: " As a client-escort situation or something else?"

A: It didn't really work out that well for that, the escort thing with me and him, but we had a lot of things in common. We were both named John, and so it was just kind of a---we just had, a rapport built up so--

Q. Okay. So about that time frame was that when you were introduced or when Dan called upon you to potentially provide escort services for John?

A: That was like at the beginning of 2006, maybe the end of 2005.

Q. Okay And was there a time in 2006 that you provided escort services to him?

A: Yeah.

Q: How did you and J.P. get along? How did you and John get along?

A: I'm sorry, I didn't hear you.

Q: How did you and John get along?

A: We got along well. We'd go to movies, things like that.

Q: Do anything else together?

A: Go out to strip clubs.

Q: Okay. Anything else:

A: At the beginning of 2006, I went and applied for a job with John at his company.

This is what happened after he met him, he went and applied it didn't work out and he quit. Tim of course still needed money. J.P. had a huge crush on him, and bought his sexual favors with money. It's that simple, the Dan story is pure fabricated bullshit. Tim didn't want the jury to know about his porn past, thinking they would be extremely prejudiced against him if they knew.

The prosecution wanted to bring it up, the Judge ruled that unless it was brought up during the direct examination, it was way too prejudicial to be brought up. Through the entire trial it was not brought up at all, not a peep or a whisper. I was shocked, I really was, so the truth of what happened that day would not be able to be brought up either. Because J.P. was blackmailing Tim over his porn star past, without bringing up how they met exactly, the blackmail couldn't be brought up, and of course it wasn't.

What was told to the jury by Tim and his lawyers was completely fabricated, and they knew it was made up. Now whose idea was this lie?

It was Tim's, for sure. Did his lawyers know it was all a lie? That's the 64-thousand dollar question. Legally a lawyer can't put their client on a witness stand knowing that whatever they say is a lie. So they can think it's a lie, but unless they really know it is, it's okay.

In a nutshell, Tim said that J.P. had cystic fibrosis, and that it was terminal, he had a huge life insurance policy. He asked Tim to help him commit suicide by giving him his gun that he (J.P.) knew he (Tim) had. He wanted to kill himself so this family would get his life insurance. His family that he never saw and barely talked to. That was the claim – that Tim brought over his gun to J.P. and he (J.P.) shot himself in the back of his head. It's hard to imagine that Tim's lawyers believed that the jury would buy any of that. However Tim, being that irrational hot head he is, insisted that version of events is the version that jury would hear and he would not relent. I think there could be a case for infective assistance of counsel on appeal. What rational attorney would go with that version? It makes no sense, and it clearly sounded like a conjured up story on the stand.

Colorado is one of the few states that allow jury questions after each witness has testified. After the direct examination and the cross examination.

The jury questions after Tim was examined by his attorney and crossed-examined by the prosecutor Diane Balkin, and reexamined by St. Clair, there was a brief intermission, so the parties could go over the jury questions. After the break Tim was back on the stand, and the questions were very telling.

The judge: "As you know, I can only ask the questions that the jurors have given to me in the fashion that they are written down. I'm not permitted to elaborate. The first question from the jury is:"

Q: How and when did J.P. learn that you owned a gun that you kept in your car?

A: When me and J.P. would go out, sometimes I would drive. I used to go to the shooting range. He saw some targets in my car and then asked me then if I had a gun.

Q: Next question, do you recall when and how you and J.P. researched making a silencer and whether or not J.P. was intoxicated during this time?

A: I researched that on the internet. It might have been at Kinko's. It have been over at a friend's house. So I don't think J.P. was actually present at the time. And I know we talked about it. I don't remember for sure if he-- I don't think that we did that together at all.

Q: Next question, did J.P. backslash John have plans to visit family for Thanksgiving?

A: I don't know.

Q: Next question, How did you know that the police would find two sets of footprints at the crime scene?

A: When I found J.P. I had stepped in some— some of his blood, so I knew that I had left footprints that time when I was there. I had seen that I had left footprints then, too, I think from some mud or something on the carpet. I don't know, it was like dust or mud.

Q: Next question, Did you and J.P. discuss that you would need to pawn his jewelry in order to benefit from this situation?

A: I did discuss this with J.P. That's why I—that was another reason that I took the safe, (which he said was empty, but had about $10 k in it). It actually had the documentation of the jewelry in it, (it didn't). It had the Rolex thing, I don't remember exactly what it was, but there was—there was paperwork in there. So, yes if I—would have pawned those, it wouldn't have been —what was the second question? I am sorry.

The Court: "Yeah Let just ask them one at a time. Did you and J.P. discuss that you would need to pawn his jewelry in order to benefit from this situation?"

A: Yes.

Q: Did you discuss that if you were to pawn the items, you might get caught since they would be known to be stolen?

A: Yes, we did.

Q: Did you ever discuss this risk with J.P."?

A: The second question, it's kind of nobody would have really known that those specific items—there was documentation for those to be stolen.

Q: The next question is, on the occasions where you would pick up J.P. and take him home due to intoxication, (he said that he would pick him from bars around Denver, after he called him drunk and drove him home, and helped him get into bed), did he ever offer you money for this service independent of whether or not you accepted it?

A: No. He never offered me money to pick him up, no. (Again he's lying, he didn't do anything with J.P. if he wasn't being paid to do it, or be there, or answer a call, he was always paid).

Q: Next question, why did you tell J.P. that he needed to drink more in order to do this on the 11th? (kill himself)

A: I don't remember exactly what time that had told him that, but I don't remember the exact reason why, but just that it was a big—

big thing that was happening. I mean, he was going to end his life. It was a major event.

Q: What did you mean by that? Oh, it's a follow-up question. Why did you tell J.P. that he needed to drink more in order to do this on the 11th? And next question for the same juror, What did you mean by that?

A: Just like I said, that was just a major event.. That's it.

Q: Next question, How was J.P.;s body positioned on the floor of the bedroom?

A: When I found him he was laying on his left side.

Q: What direction?

A: His head was toward the closet and his feet were towards the –the-- to the dresser on the east side of the room.

When I watched him answer these questions, it was so clear to me that he was lying, I looked over at the jury and it looked as if they knew it too, and these questions only cemented that belief for me.

Q: On his back or stomach?

A: H was on his side.

Q: Next question: Was money exchanged for picking him, J.P., up and taking him home?

A: He gave me money, but not necessarily for picking him up.

That's true, J.P. gave Tim money for having sex with him, for Tim this was all about money, that's it.

Q: Next question: In the video to Christina (Tim's pregnant girlfriend, a video tape of a jail house visit was shown to the jury) you tell her you were going to turn yourself in or go back across the border but got scared at seeing the three officers standing there and thought they were there for you. So you went back to the hotel. Is this true or did you make this up to tell Christina?

A: This was true.

No it wasn't, he didn't go back to the hotel he turned himself in, some of the lies he told were seemingly for no reason.

Q: Next question, At what point on the day of the shooting did you go out to your vehicle and retrieve your gun? Why did you bring it back into the house?

A: After J.P.--I am sorry, what was the question again?

I believe while the judge was re-reading the jury question, Tim was thinking up his next lie. This question is based off a lie that he told. He brought the gun into the house, he didn't have to get it.

Q: At what point on the day of the shooting did you bring did you go to your vehicle to retrieve the gun? Why did you bring it back in the house?

A: This was after J.P. and I had both decided that yes, this is what was going to happen. I brought it back in so it could happen – the suicide.

Q: On the day of the shooting at what point was J.P. first aware that you had your gun with you? What was his reaction?

A: I told him that I had it in the car. As far as when he had it—when I had it with me was when I brought it from the car, and I don't remember what his reaction was. I know he looked at it.

Q: Next question, When you were interviewed by Detective Lopez on November 16, 2006, why did you never mention to him the events of Saturday 11 were preplanned in an attempt to end J.P.'s life?

The jury meant that J.P planned on committing suicide on that day. The obvious answer is because that's a lie. Here is how Tim answered that question.

A: That is what he wanted, basically.

Q; Why didn't you mention the event was supposed to look like a robbery gone bad?

A: At that point I was still covering for J.P. He said his family was going to get his life insurance, and I didn't think anybody would believe that he actually had killed himself. I didn't know a lot of things at the time.

Oh like perhaps J.P. didn't even have any life insurance, he didn't know it when he murdered him, or when he said on the stand that J.P. committed suicide. He found that out when he was cross examined.

Q: What was your motive for bringing your gun into J. P.'s house on the date of his death?

That is kind of a silly question in lieu of the fact that he already lied and said a few times, that it was so J.P. could use his gun to kill himself.

A: To go through with the assisted suicide.

Q: Did J.P. shot himself while wearing handcuffs?

A. No.

J.P. Kelso had been handcuffed, at some point, and the cuffs were found on one of his wrists. This isn't even a good lie, it's like he wanted to be found guilty. He really didn't but from this preposterous lie he told on the stand, it certainly seemed like he wanted to be found guilty.

Q: Next question: Did you have any reason to believe you were listed as a beneficiary of Kelso's life insurance policy?

A: I did not.

Q: Next question, What did you do stand to gain from making J.P.'s suicide look like a murder?

A: J.P. gave me the things from his house.

That was his answer, he murdered him, and he took whatever he wanted and then took his girlfriend to the Comedy Store later that night and laughed the night away. That is very chilling in my opinion. However he sugar coated what he did and why he did, that picture of him sitting there laughing with his girlfriend never left my head.

Q: Next question, After you heard gunshot and realized J.P. shot himself, why not just call the police?

Tim's story was that J.P. shot himself in his bedroom and Tim was in the kitchen area downstairs.

A: At first when I had tried to revive him, I had blood all over myself, and with the DNA stuff like that, I had a major freakout. I didn't know what to do.

Q: When you went to J.P's house on Saturday, 11 back slash 11 were you planning on robbing him?

A: No I wasn't.

Q: Why didn't you tell the police in Arizona during your interview that J.P. shot himself?

A: Again it was just A, I didn't think anyone would believe me; B, he still told that his family was to get his life insurance. I was still covering for him.

Q: If you were afraid of getting arrested, as you testified, why did you turn yourself in?

A: I am sorry can you repeat the question.

Q: If you were afraid of getting arrested, as you testified, why did you turn yourself in?

Intended for Mature Audiences/Donna Thomas

A. Well I was in the National Guard at that time (he wasn't) and I didn't know at that time if I was going to fall under the Uniform Code of Military Justice. You can still be put to death for small felonies and things like that, (you can't) And I figured if there were—if I were to get arrested by the military police, that I could be hung or something like that. I didn't want to do that, so that's why I was trying to—at least, if I was going to be convicted, I would have rather had it done with Denver rather than face a military tribunal. I mean, just with m past and things like that, it would been very bad for me to go military jail in the first place. And, then, the second thing would have been you know, like I said, I don't know what they would try to do, like, hang me. I just didn't know so---

it was hard to listen to him like that, I'm just about positive that his family — all of them — knew everything he was saying on the stand was a lie. Pretty much every sentence, everything he said was damning to him.

Q: Why did you not initially tell your mom and your sister and investigators, etc, that Mr. Kelso had committed suicide?

A: Again, I didn't think anyone would actually believe me. And I was like I said, I was —I was still covering for J.P. I thought the other path would be the best way to go.

Q: After you met J.P. back slash John, approximately how many time do you remember J.P. visiting his family?

That was one of the best questions the jury asked in my opinion. Since Tim said that reason J.P. wanted to commit suicide was that the family he barely spoke to could get the life insurance that he didn't even have. Makes perfect sense right?

A: I actually went with J.P. one time to the Cherry Creek Mall. There's a video store here, video game store there, video game store and he had – I think it was ---this was a long time ago, like three years ago. Ia m pretty sure it was a nephew he actually bought a game system for. I think a PSP or something like that. But he had bought that and some video games for the nephew that day. So he went the next day, I think it was his nephew's birthday party. I was supposed to with him, but I couldn't go with him, but I couldn't go.

He had so much trouble answering that question, because it was all made up!

Q: How many times did J.P. talk to you about his family in the last three months of his life?

A: Can you repeat the question?

Q: How many times or how often did J.P. speak with you about his family in the last three months before he died.

He was thinking up a good lie to tell that, it was clear from looking at him.

A: I don't know exactly how many times, but he did talk about his mom, and that were kind of estranged from each other. But—so we talked about that. (YES HE REALLY ANSWERED THE QUESTION THAT WAY!) I don't remember when his nephew's birthday was. I think it was in the summer of 2006. I am pretty sure it was his nephew. So probably we talked about his home several times times. That Wednesday (he was killed on a Saturday) I told him to call his mom if was really going to go through with this just to give her a call, and so ten times before.

Even with that lie he told his own lie did not recount ten times.

Q: Can you name the specific family members that J.P. told you would benefit from his life insurance policy?

A: No, He just said that his friends and family would benefit, and family would benefit. He didn't say anyone specifically.

I visited Tim in jail shortly after he gave this piece of testimony, and I said, "hey, are you sure J.P. did put m me down as a registered recipient of his insurance policy?" He said, "Fuck you!"

He just lied and lied some more, non-stop, I think if the truth would have come out, about his porno star past, and his pregnant girlfriend and his hopes of playing it straight and being a good father, and J.P. trying to systematically destroy his life by keeping him at his beck and call, at least one jury member would have took some pity on him, and maybe hung the jury, but with these type of fairy tale lies he had no chance.

Five days later after Tim's dreadful appearance on the witness stand. July 9th ,the jury filed back into the courtroom. They had a verdict they told the judge, and looked down as they took their seats in the jury box. They weren't smiling and didn't look up as the verdict was read by the judge.

Tim was found guilty of first degree premeditated murder, he was sentenced to life without parole. He looked down and back to the courtroom,

I just looked at him shaking my head, it was a very final outcome for a very young man of 28, that's all he was, not even 30; today he's 33, and his life is all laid out for him. For a person that hated structure, that's all he has now.

Intended for Mature Audiences/Donna Thomas

Home these days for Timothy John Boham is a Arkansas Valley Correctional Facility in Crowley, Colorado. He is relegated to his tiny cell 23 hours a day to protect Tim from his own porno star past. Tim, John, Marcus is more often referred to as Inmate Number 146418.

In a recent conversation I had with him, he said, "I thought doing porno with a bunch of sick people was bad, and it was bad. This place is bad and sick and full of sick people. This place is so bad, it's beyond bad. No one should ever have to know of a place like this."

Tim's mother and step-father sill live in Aurora and make the almost 3 hour drive each way to the penitentiary to visit Tim, his sister visits but very infrequently. As of this writing Tim is 33, he spent his best years locked away in a tiny hole. He has nothing but a pile of regrets and has nothing but time to think about all of his regrets. No habeas corpus has been filed yet, as most legal experts say that Tim nailed his own coffin, and now, after the fact, the coffin can't be opened. He says that life behind bars, for an inmate like him is even more hellish due to his isolation and the endless hours of nothingness. What could have been? We can't ever know now, sadly.

Tim's young daughter Jasmine – who is now 13 – was adopted by the man who co-owned Maxim Talent, Rob Lail. Tim said of Rob, he was a monster "that started a campaign against me early on, to steal my child from me." Tim's family didn't try to gain custody of the youngest family member, and that now is a great source of pain.

Intended for Mature Audiences/Donna Thomas

Some say Tim is getting everything he deserves and then some, and that no tears will be shed. Perhaps, though, some tears for the little real innocent victim, Jasmine who lost so very much..........

Meet our Author

Donna Thomas

Donna Thomas, has a jurist doctorate degree, and writes extensively on true crime and pop culture. She has interviewed dozens of high profile criminals including Ted Bundy, Richard Ramirez, Charles Manson, John Gotti, Henry

Hill, Scott Peterson and many others. She regularly appears on radio and television as an expert commentator on true crime.

www.ingramcontent.com/pod-product-compliance
Lightning Source LLC
Chambersburg PA
CBHW070556100426
42744CB00006B/302